Honoring the Moment in Young Children's Lives

HONORING THE MOMENT
IN YOUNG CHILDREN'S LIVES

Observation, Documentation, and Reflection

RON GRADY

Redleaf Press®
www.redleafpress.org
800-423-8309

Published by Redleaf Press
10 Yorkton Court
St. Paul, MN 55117
www.redleafpress.org

First edition 2024
Cover design by Louise OFarrell
Cover photographs by Ron Grady and Lauren Rouatt
Interior design by Michelle Lee Lagerroos
Typeset in Baskerville URW, Verveine, and Futura PT
Interior photos by Ron Grady
Interior illustrations by ©pandaclub23/Adobe Stock, ©Twins Design Studio/Adobe Stock, and ©Kat Ka/Adobe Stock

Printed in the United States of America
31 30 29 28 27 26 25 24   1 2 3 4 5 6 7 8

Library of Congress Cataloging-in-Publication Data
Names: Grady, Ron, author.
Title: Honoring the moment in young children's lives : observation, documentation,
    and reflection / by Ron Grady.
Description: First edition. | St. Paul, MN : Redleaf Press, 2024. |
    Includes bibliographical references and index. | Summary: "Deftly weaving anthropology,
    sociology, psychology, and theories of education, Honoring the Moment in Young Children's Lives
    invites us to remake our image of the child and truly appreciate children for who they are at this
    time. Take the next step in observing and documenting young children and embrace the role of
    researcher, an ethnographer with unique and privileged proximity to children who takes a close-up
    look and uses that deep knowledge to advocate for children's needs and their right to live their lives
    engaged in deep inquiry and self-directed, meaningful play"-- Provided by publisher.
Identifiers: LCCN 2024001066 (print) | LCCN 2024001067 (ebook) | ISBN
    9781605548135 (paperback) | ISBN 9781605548142 (ebook)
Subjects: LCSH: Children--Research. | Children--Psychological aspects. |
    Children--Sociological aspects.
Classification: LCC HQ767.85 .G69 2024 (print) | LCC HQ767.85 (ebook) |
    DDC 305.23--dc23/eng/20240409
LC record available at https://lccn.loc.gov/2024001066
LC ebook record available at https://lccn.loc.gov/2024001067

Printed on acid-free paper

To Karin Sandstrand, Clare Loughran, Danielle Lobell, Abby Bradford, Suzie Fowler, and Lauren Rouatt—my teacher brain trust.

To the Dandelions, Greenie Gardeners, Maples, Bluejays, Crawfish, and Green Dragonflies—for loving, learning, and creating with me—and for inviting me in.

Contents

Acknowledgments

A huge thanks to Melissa, my amazing editor, for believing in me and patiently waiting until these ideas were baked enough to be ready to assemble into a book!

To my husband, Josh, for giving me the space to write, listening to my tangents, and asking the hard questions all along the way. I love you!

To my mom and my sister, Lena and Ke'Imba, for showing me what it means to be a dedicated educator whose work is rooted in care, in love, and in the belief that each and every child matters.

Introduction

I love museums. In fact, I'd even go as far as to say that they are some of my favorite places in the entire world. They are physical and psychological spaces where time collides with itself—spaces where we, in the present moment, encounter artifacts rendered by hands and minds from across space, time, and experience. I can spend hours gazing at beautiful and challenging artwork; creations woven from soft textiles, slathered on with thick oils, gently brushed with organic tempera. I am drawn, too, to pristinely printed photographs; sculptures, suspended or sturdy upon a hefty base; and simple assemblages of artifact, carefully placed, perhaps, in an elevated glass box in the middle of the floor. But, without fail, what captures my attention most consistently are the depictions of other human beings—especially, perhaps unsurprisingly, children.

Often children are depicted in idealized imagery—bundles swaddled in gauzy fabric, running through fields in bucolic settings, smiling, holding hands, in harmony. But of course there are other moments—moments that are just as, if not more, real than those we like to see that make it into many popular depictions of idealized children and childhoods.

This book wonders: What is possible when we look at children in ways that go beyond how we wish we saw them? What is happening with children? What do they think, know, want, and desire from life? How can we, through attentive observation of children's play and relationship, through the intentional gathering of their stories, words, and artifacts, construct a more authentic picture of children and childhood? And having gathered these representations, how can we use them to invite change?

This book is grounded in critical childhoods theories, articulated powerfully by Haeny Yoon and Tran Templeton in a 2019 article, "The Practice of Listening to Children," looking at how adults, even those of us who are well meaning, often subordinate children's intentions to our own ends. As recently as 2023, Clio Stearns invites those working with children to consider, *really* consider, how the images we have of children and the ways of interacting with children that are a result of these images impact our moment-to-moment relationships with them. Similar sentiments have been and are being expressed by practitioners Vivian

Paley, Deb Curtis and Margie Carter, and others. In conversation with scholars like Yoon, Templeton, and Stearns, and with Paley, Curtis, and Carter—and a few others whom you'll meet shortly—I attempt to articulate an answer.

This book is an endeavor to both assemble and share my own image of the child as it exists in this moment in time. It is an image gathered over undergraduate years working with young children in research and applied settings at Stanford University's Bing Nursery School in California. It is an image developed over years of living, learning, and creating alongside children in classrooms—indoors and outdoors and in more traditional, entirely play-based, and in-between types of settings. It is an image developed alongside colleagues within each of my workplaces and with my master's degree cohort at the Erikson Institute. It is an image refined within the writing-filled pages of at least a dozen journals, innumerable scraps of paper filled with hastily written notes, arrows, and sketches (my own and children's), more than ten thousand photographs, honed as I engaged with children's drawings, maps, and memories. It is an image that is always and forever incomplete—and this incompletion is a great joy. It means that this book, the images that inform it, and the image that it coalesces into are also an invitation for you, reader, to create, interrogate, revise, and re-create your own.

In the course of this book, I present documentation as an act of ethnographic fieldwork and explore the processes around gathering and curating the stories, artifacts, and examples of experience that will effectively and impactfully illuminate the processes unfolding in children's lives. As we adopt our anthropological, ethnographic lens, I also invite us to wrestle with the tensions inherent in our work. Just like the work of anthropologists, so, too, as adults working with children, our work is not free from bias. Like anthropology, education is a field rife with contradiction and exists as it does as the result of many difficult and painful histories whose ramifications go far beyond us and will, quite likely, outlive us. Holding these in mind, nonetheless, we attempt our curation project with gentle intention. We search for artifacts, stories, and examples and, once we find them, respectfully hold them in our hands and arrange them with care.

However, as with any exhibition, it is important to conceptualize our work as an act of storytelling and narration. We are agents in this work. We are also fallible. There are things that we see and things we do not—there are, perhaps, people whom we see and whom we do not. Any act of curation is also an act of exclusion and excision. Whose likenesses are foregrounded and whose images, intentional or not, do not appear at all?

Another crucial question involves how curators wrestle with the decisions that must, ultimately, be made. Which stories remain after careful gathering and exclusion? How and to what extent can the new narrative retain the meaning of the original creators or their subjects, and at the same time connect meaningfully to the lives of the present-day viewers—to the lives of those of us walking through the cavernous halls of a great museum or ambling slowly along the edges of an intimate gallery? These are questions that aren't easily answered, and they are not meant to be. However, as you engage with this book, with the practices of documentation explored here, and as you try on and sit with the framing I invite you into, I encourage you to hold these questions in your heart and mind.

ABOUT THIS BOOK

Documenting children's lives is a privilege and obligation that at the same time comes along with a lot of questions. Typically these include the when, how, and what of documenting and how to document with an eye toward standards, norms, and expectations. This book, while aware of these questions, is not about these topics, at least not explicitly. Rather, this book focuses on what might happen, what can happen, if we dare to view children's lives as a series of rich moments, all of which are valuable and all of which deserve close attention and consideration. What becomes possible—in our practice, in our classrooms, in our schools and communities, and in *children*—when this happens?

This book seeks to invite you into a sustained practice of deep reflection that extends above and beyond what may be typically asked as educators. Reflecting on the work we do with children, on who children are, on what children need, and on the ways that children are making meaning in the world is an essential and indispensable piece of our work as early childhood educators. By engaging in sustained reflection, we become ever more alive to the intricacy and vibrancy of children's worlds and prepare ourselves to be better educators and advocates for these young humans who spend so much time with us in community.

One of the central pieces of reflection is, as the title of this book suggests, documentation. Documenting children's experiences means that we spend time taking a closeup look at what has happened or is happening, thinking about how we can respond both in the moment and beyond.

This book is divided into six chapters, each of which explores a central component of what it means to document children's lives through this perspective.

In chapter 1, "Discerning and Reforming: Imagery of Children and Childhood," I invite readers to consider: Who, really, is a child? I also wonder who are *we*—the adults who work with children? Grounding ourselves in an image of children and of educators is a key point of departure, as our images of ourselves and the humans with whom we work are the foundation from which our practices of observation, documentation, and reflection practices unfold.

In chapter 2, "The Inexhaustible Richness of the Day," I invite us to consider what might shift in our practices and perspectives if we think of the mundane moments of our days as filled with rich significance for children—and as deeply informative for the adults who work with them. I insist not only that children are already experiencing their daily lives as deeply meaningful but also that when adults embrace this perspective, it opens up new possibilities for connection and inquiry, creating opportunities for our documentation to take on new dimensions.

In chapter 3, "Uniquely Proximate Positioning," I explore the implications of the closeup nature of teachers' daily experiences with children. I suggest that teachers' proximity to children affords opportunities to know things and connect threads that would be impossible for other adults in their lives to connect. Does this grant teachers access to children's voices and experiences, and if so, how and to what extent? What does this unique access mean for the way we view, think about, speak about, and present information about children?

Chapter 4, "Lens and Frame: Documentation as Ethnography," draws parallels between documentation and ethnography, inviting educators to view themselves as ethnographers of children's lives, relationships, and cultures within classroom spaces. I invite educators to embrace multiple modes of understanding and building meaning with children and to consider the implications of their work and framing on their images of children and childhood.

In chapter 5, "Advocating for Children's Lives," I share stories of ways that using documentation gathered using an ethnographic lens supported my efforts at advocating for children within broader school and community spaces. In particular, I consider how documenting through an ethnographic lens might be a valuable tool in conversations with colleagues, administrators, and others invested in children's well-being, in that it invites them to consider the implications of their practices, policies, and dispositions in a new way. I look at four case studies across various school contexts and ages.

Chapter 6, "Learning from Ethnographies," is devoted to considering what it is possible to learn from our ethnographically oriented documentation. It wonders what questions this perspective invites educators into, and suggests a few concrete practices to stimulate their practice.

From wherever you are and whatever your prior experiences may be, I invite you to enter into this book as you would a conversation with a valued colleague: bring your curiosity, agreements, disagreements, wonders, and enthusiasms here. They are welcome. I hope this book is one you visit and revisit, gleaning new insights and asking new questions as you and your children engage in the daily beauties of life—together.

Chapter 1

Discerning and Reforming: Imagery of Children and Childhood

□ □ □ □

INTRODUCTION: WHAT DO YOU THINK ABOUT CHILDREN?

The way that we think about children, how they are, who they are, what they can do, their dispositions—these are the cornerstones of our connection with them that inform every single thing we do. For this reason, in the opening chapter of this text on children's lives, I invite us to reflect on our images of children. What images currently and previously have dominated our society and our field of early care and learning—or, we might more accurately say, our field of early collaboration, co-creativity, and co-inquiry? How have these images come to be?

In the first half of this chapter, we explore existing philosophies and perspectives, dipping our toes into the approaches, philosophies, and disciplines that have influenced contemporary notions of childhood. We begin with the contributions of the Reggio approach and its groundbreaking perspective on children before turning our sights to some of the contributions of the social sciences like sociology and anthropology, after which we consider a short but influential list of educational philosophers. What, we ask, do these frameworks have to offer us as we think about children and childhood? What might it look like to build on these notions?

In the second half of this chapter, we turn our gazes inward, reflecting on the ways our own experiences have influenced our images of childhood and what these experiences and their resultant images mean for us as early childhood educators—as adults working with young children.

~

WHAT EVEN IS A CHILD?

If you are reading this book, it is likely that you already have some idea of what a child is (a small or young human being, a pupil to be taught, a gift to be treasured, an enigma to be figured out, or . . .). You also have an idea of what a child tends to be like—curious, perhaps. Innocent? Cunning? Furthermore, you probably have some idea of what a child or children tend to (or tend *not* to) be able to do. Perhaps you work with children, you have your own children, or you know a friend with a child or two. Wherever you fall, I invite you to take a moment to bring a child or group of children to mind. Then reflect again: What is a child like? What do you believe about children? If you find yourself near a journal and a pen, now would be an ideal time to take a few moments and make some bullet points about what comes to mind when you think of the word *child*. Below are a few quotations about children and childhood—what do you think of them?

> *Children are "powerful, active, competent protagonists of their own growth" (Edwards, Gandini, and Forman 2012, 150).*

> *Children are "active, creative social agents who produce their own unique children's cultures" (Corsaro 2015, 3).*

> *Children are "expensive little cherubs" (Lancy 2015, 27).*

As you read the phrases, did anything come to mind that you might add, challenge, or qualify? The way you answer begins to tell you about your image of children.

DEFINING AN IMAGE OF THE CHILD

The Reggio approach provides a rather complete framework for discussing and conceptualizing children. The result of a grassroots restructuring of an educational system in postwar Italy, the approach is now world-renowned for the respect it accords children; the importance it places on observing, documenting, and dialoguing with children; and the way the ideas that are borne of this close relationship extend beyond classrooms and into the communities within which they are nestled. The approach of Reggio Emilia, alongside other learner/child-centered pedagogical approaches, understands children to be "powerful, active, competent protagonists of their own growth" (Edwards, Gandini, and Forman 2012, 150). This book also adopts this orientation.

One of the many gifts of the Reggio approach is its language around the "image of the child." Succinctly, an *image of the child* refers to what one thinks about children. As the exercise above perhaps reiterated, every adult has an image of the child. Your image of the child, regardless of whether this is the first time you have reflected upon it, defines and determines the way you approach every interaction you have with children.

For example, if you imagine children as vulnerable, danger prone, and needing to be corralled and taught the "right" way to be, the rituals, routines, and invitations you engage in and present to your children will look far different than they do in a classroom where children are viewed as creative, interesting, curious seekers who have a right to pursue their own interests.

In addition to the Reggio approach, formal academic disciplines pertaining to education, such as the social sciences of anthropology and sociology, also have their own images of children that inform the dominant images taken in this book. These images, and those of the educational philosophers, researchers, and social scientists focused on development who have espoused them, offer images of children that, you will likely notice, have found their ways into adults' existing images of young humans.

The disciplines of anthropology and sociology conceive of childhood as a socially constructed life stage that varies immensely in its materiality and lived experience. This means that what a child does, what is expected of children, and what children's daily lives look like are far from uniform in different societies and cultures. While a globalized world renders many humans more able than ever to share ideas and perspectives about this common life stage, it remains that the experiences and material cultures of children across time and geography have been, and are still, heavily influenced by the circumstances, affordances, and constraints of an individual child's family and community.

Anthropology: Children as Cultural Replicators

Indeed, children's participation within particular communities of care—that children can, do, and are encouraged to participate in—is an idea at the core of much of the anthropology of childhood (Lancy 2015). Barbara Rogoff (2003, 80) emphasizes children's participation in the activities of their cultural communities, which are defined by Rogoff as "groups of people who have some common and continuing organization, values, understanding, history, and practices." Each of these communities—*cultural communities* that share norms and ways of thinking broadly and *communities of care* that are more immediate members of community such as caregivers and family systems—provide models for children and invite them into some degree of active participation. With cultural communities, this comes through general influence, and with communities of care, through the ways that they filter cultural norms and give meaning to them through intimate interactions and relationships. Through this active participation in these often-overlapping circles, Rogoff emphasizes, children are inducted holistically into their cultures—they are able to internalize the values, practices, ideas, and perspectives of those in their cultural circles.

In turn, these cultural differences determine everything from how and to what degree children are the sole responsibilities of their biological parents versus a collective of adults, to whether children are coddled or are carried (and how) and how children are spoken to. Questions such as whether children are capable of making their own decisions and how intensely they need to be protected from the outside world vary across cultures. Who a child is, then, depends on how their culture views them, and how their culture views them influences the way a culture answers or even conceives of the question of who they are.

Children, in this view, are savvy learners who expend significant energy learning, honing, and seeking to replicate culture. However, some scholars believe that children are not merely actively being inducted into their cultures but also influencing and codeveloping them. That is to say, children are not just learners but also creative improvisers of cultural life.

Sociology: Children as Creative Improvisers

Sociologist William Corsaro calls childhood "a period in which children live their lives and a category of part of society," adding that "it is a permanent structural category" in our societies (Corsaro 2015, 30). Said another way, this means that childhood is both the actual reality of being a young human, and it is also always something that, in all societies, is considered separate from adults. Whatever particular age range it encompasses, whatever its obligations and characteristics, across time and place, there is always a time of life that is considered *childhood*. The sociology of childhood as we now know it came into its own following the United Nations Convention on the Rights of the Child in 1989. This convention advocated for children's full participation in matters concerning their lives. As such, it may come as little surprise that the sociology of childhood as currently conceived in many Western contexts positions children as active participants in the processes of cultural creation.

Corsaro, the pioneering thought leader in what is often called a "new" sociological vision of childhood, emphasizes children's participation in cultural processes. In this framework, children are mutually influential participants in parallel and intersecting cultures. Children participate in adult and dominant cultures (such as family or school cultures); children create their own cultures with one another (their peer cultures); and each of these cultures, dominant and peer, influence one another.

As educators, we are especially interested in what Corsaro terms *interpretive reproduction*—which is, at its core, the ways that children take elements of adult culture and reproduce them with their own unique flair, in interactions, play, ways of speaking, and more. Interpretive reproduction is what we are witnessing when a child dresses and rocks a baby doll while singing it to sleep, when a group of children pretend to be a bat family in a tree, or when a group of children inhabit the roles of superhero and supervillain. Each of these elements of play involves a familiar cultural practice or script that is being enacted in a unique way by the child or group of children.

These moments are happening constantly, and they are the things that often bring a smile to our adult faces and, at the same time, convey to us some of the things that children are internalizing most saliently about what it means to be a member of a group/culture. Children, this shows us, are creative and complex humans.

Psychology: Childhood on Trajectory

The contributions of the field of psychology to the images of children, particularly in Western society, cannot be overstated. Children, the field suggests, behave in predictable ways and can be influenced by their social and educational environments.

The influential Jean Piaget dedicated many of his efforts to observations of his own children, which left him convinced that children are constantly building on a set of skills and competencies at which they succeed in more-or-less predictable sequences. Lev Vygotsky paved the way for developmentalists to conceptualize childhood as embedded within a social and cultural world, where children learn their way into society through scaffolded participation. Countless contemporary developmental psychologists work at the intersections of social and cognitive psychology, among many other domains, and have demonstrated that children begin with the bases of many competencies—that is, children do not come into the world as blank slates. It seems that children come into the world wired to mirror facial expressions and to hold ideas about agents, about their own intentions, and about who might help or hinder them from moving toward those intentions within the first few months of life. From early ages, young children also have expectations about who likes or connects with or is related to whom, where a particular person falls along or within a social continuum or hierarchy, how social relationships are influenced by features such as linguistic background, and more. Children are already making inferences about objects, intuiting what objects might be for (for example, making music), how it works (it makes music when pressing one button but not another), and with ideas about how (or not) to make it work efficiently—and the list goes on. Children, psychology agrees, do not need to be filled up with knowledge.

So, taken together, what we end up with is an understanding that a child is born with the building blocks of many awarenesses and many ways of seeking information and interaction. At the same time, children are learning about and also bringing their own unique experiences and cognitive architectures to every situation they are part of. These, then, all interact to produce the child's experience within the world.

These social scientific disciplines were influenced by and conversant with a variety of educational philosophies taking root across the United States and Europe throughout the twentieth century. Children, this reaffirms, have always been persons of interest within a society. While the next section reviews a few educational philosophies that have been especially influential to early education in the United States (the country from which I am writing), it is by no means an exhaustive review, neither in the persons it examines nor in the method of exploring the ideas set forth by them. Nonetheless, I hope it serves to advance an understanding of the ways in which any image of the child we have is rooted in the various ideas and understandings of culture and the result of centuries of ongoing and evolving discourse on the topic of childhood. As you read, I invite you to wonder:

How do each of these images of children and childhood look today?

Which images do we, do *I*, hold on to?

Which have I let go?

The Images of Educational Thinkers

Educational philosophers have long offered their perspectives on what a child is and how a child experiences the world. In all cases, each educational philosopher was working within a cultural context that had specific anthropological and cultural perspectives on childhood. Given the scope of the current work, we will focus on only a few of these educational philosophers, wondering if—and if so, in what ways—their ideas of childhood still yield influence in our work today.

In *Preschool Education in America*, Barbara Beatty (1995), professor emerita of education at Wellesley College, provides a detailed account of how preschool education in the United States came, at least in part, to adopt its current form. She notes that Johann Heinrich Pestalozzi (1746–1827) was "the first European educator to develop pedagogical methods consciously derived from experimentation with real children" through reading the philosopher Jean-Jacques Rousseau and working with Rousseau's philosophies grounded in the value of hands-on, real-life experiences (Beatty 1995, 10). Pestalozzi invited children to encounter ideas, concepts, and principles in multiple ways before ever giving names to them. Beatty also reminds us that Pestalozzi was a novelist, who in his written work emphasized the valuable role of meaningful everyday experiences—of particular import for the poor of his time who may not have had access to formal educational spaces—in fostering skills and dispositions in both academic and aesthetic domains. Our ideas, then, about the growth, learning, and development of children have been influenced by and are grounded in historical forms of communication and creativity and in relationships between social and economic classes, and they are a result of the cross-pollination of philosophical ideas.

Pestalozzi laid a groundwork upon which others continued to build. Educational philosopher Friedrich Fröbel (1782–1852) is responsible for kindergarten as is currently conceived. In the later nineteenth century, Maria Montessori (1870–1952) reiterated the critical value of the very earliest years of a child's life, suggesting that through the systematic facilitation of experiences within a structured, responsive environment, children could build upon and extend their abilities. She wrote that "education is not what the teacher gives [but rather] a natural process spontaneously carried out by the human individual. It is acquired not by listening to words, but by experiences upon the environment" (Montessori 1949, 5).

Montessori also advocated for integration between children's experiences in early education and the practical social and emotional experiences that are key components of children's lives. Her methodological approach is heavily influenced by the theories of the stages of development then prevalent in the field—theories that break down childhood into easily interpretable components while still attempting to maintain an awareness of the flexibility inherent in young children's abilities, interests, and priorities.

THE STANCE OF THIS BOOK: CHILDREN AS FULL HUMAN BEINGS

Today, in early childhood education, childhood contexts exist at the nexus of the features of these ideas from anthropology, sociology, psychology, and the philosophy of education. We are, for example, highly aware of the individual trajectories of children and of the undeniable role of culture, context, and society on experience such that every child exists within entirely unique circumstances. In addition, we now have centuries of research—qualitative and quantitative—that informs us of children's predictable progress throughout particular stages of understanding the world in many dimensions, with many studies able to examine the finer points of this understanding (for example, that children know what they should do at a given age, can only express it at a slightly later age, and do not actually do it until an even later age). The intersection of these ideas, and our ability to hold each of them simultaneously, has informed educational frameworks that seek both to standardize and to disrupt the ways educators approach their work.

Our images of children and childhood are not neutral, should not be assumed to be universal, and must very much be continually reappraised in light of what we know about their origins and how they relate to our current knowledge.

Some Notes on Educational Frameworks

Many organizations, governing bodies, and constituencies, especially in the past few decades, have articulated frameworks of early learning and development that offer guidelines to support educators in identifying and furthering optimal development along a variety of dimensions. Very often, individual child care contexts, preschools, and so on will have their own hyperspecific versions of these frameworks that are a mixture of other higher-level and/or more specific frameworks. While interesting and valuable, for the purposes of our current discussion we are less interested in what the frameworks say explicitly and more interested in what they reveal that we, as individuals invested in children's lives, believe to be true about children, how they are, and how they experience life in the world.

In my context (living in the United States), many early childhood frameworks emphasize the multilayered nature of well-being in young children. These frameworks may encourage educators to center socioemotional learning and to acknowledge and account for the ways that context, culture, and society influence the experiences of their children before, outside of, and within school. For example, *Developmentally Appropriate Practice in Early Childhood Programs* by the

National Association for the Education of Young Children (2022) insists that educators working with young children and families consider the commonalities young children are experiencing, their individuality, and the context in which their development unfolds.

Given the evolution of the social and psychological sciences on childhood and the development of the educational sciences, the advent of these frameworks and their increasing emphasis on context and intersectionality are, perhaps, unsurprising. What is important to note is that these frameworks comprise central components of our image of the child because they suggest, among other things, what optimal development looks like, when and how we should expect to see it, and which domains of development we should prioritize. Each of these assertions, in turn, influences the ways that we view each individual child we interact with.

Each of these frameworks also leaves us with an image of children as complex human beings whose well-being we are obligated to actively seek. Each of these also acknowledges children as human beings who are in conversation with the world around them and each of the smaller worlds with which they interact directly on a daily basis.

In this book, I work from a perspective that views children as full human beings.

Along with many of the educators, scholars, theorists, and philosophers mentioned in the previous sections, this book also asserts that children are capable, competent, active, intellectually curious, and able to/endowed with the rights to pursue their own ends and interest (see also United Nations 2009). Just as most young adults do not spend their days focused exclusively on aspects of their lives that will promote health in their old age, it is important that children are accorded this same privilege. To focus exclusively on a child's progress toward the goals of later childhood, middle childhood, or adolescence or adulthood is a mistake. A significant aim of the current work is to show just *why* this would be a mistake by emphasizing the richness of children's lives. The foremost implication of this line of thinking is that children's lives, as they are lived *in the moment*, matter. Childhood is important for children *now.*

In the above sections, we have explored some of the ways that our image of children generally (and the image of the child that this book adopts) has been influenced by certain educational philosophies and by the social and educational sciences. In the next, we will consider another hugely influential aspect of our images of children: our own personal experiences.

THE ROLE OF PERSONAL EXPERIENCES

Though mentioned above, it bears repetition: Every one of us has an image of the child, whether or not we have given it conscious thought. This image is reflected in everything we do during the day: how we interact with children, prepare environments for them to inhabit, respond to their creativities, inquiries, and improvisations on our plans—all of these things, each and every one of them, reflects a particular image of the child.

As we continue to identify our current image of children and its roots, we must take a look at our own experiences. Therefore, in this next section we consider how our images of children and childhood have been formed by (1) our own childhoods, (2) the contexts in which we have encountered children, and (3) our pedagogical formation (formal or informal).

Consideration 1: What Was Your Childhood Like?

Before you read this section, take a moment to think: What was your childhood like?

The inescapable, undeniable reality is that our own childhoods influence the ways that we see children in our adult lives. For example, have you or someone you know ever referenced their own childhood in speaking about their hopes or fears for children in their care? That might look, for example, like someone saying, "I just want to give my child everything I never had," or an educator declaring, "I want to be the teacher I needed when I was their age." This is, at least in my experience, a common refrain—and one that I think has its own benefits and difficulties as a frame of reference that are beyond the scope of this chapter. What I am trying to emphasize is that the ways we felt emotionally as children influence our relationship to childhood now. Our past experiences with elements of childhood material culture influence our relationship to childhood. Whether we felt prioritized, dismissed, pressured, or celebrated by the adults, children, and others in our lives all influence our relationship to childhood.

Once you begin to think about it, it's hard not to see how so much of our relationship to children and childhood is influenced by our experience. Imagine—how might your interactions with a child look different depending on whether you were able to express your emotions freely or told to keep a "stiff upper lip"? How might your previous positive, challenging, or negative experiences in athletic or academic pursuits, in social pursuits, and so on contribute to the foundation of the way you think about childhood? Our parents and families of origin also influence our concepts of childhood by providing a frame of reference for us. However, our experiences of our own childhoods are not the only things that influence the ways we view children. Whatever our foundation, it is constantly being built and being revised by what we know about children and childhood.

Consideration 2: In What Contexts Have You Encountered Children?

Our understanding of children and childhood is also influenced by the contexts in which we have encountered children. I invite you to take a moment to reflect on the spaces, places, and environments in which you have interacted with and observed children.

If, for example, your primary experiences with young children have been in a classroom setting, then it is likely that your image of children has been informed by coexisting with them in a space full of peers and materials for exploration, and that provides certain freedoms and also places certain constraints on their behavior. Alternatively, if your primary experiences with young children have been in an informal education setting where you encounter a broad range of children for short bursts of time as they are engaged in focused work with well-outlined steps, sequences, and a highly defined goal, your image of children will be different.

Every context, especially every educational context, invites a child to show up in a different way. To illustrate this point, I'd like you to imagine the following two classrooms. As you read them and the picture clarifies in your mind, reflect on these two questions:

1. What does this environment say about what a child needs in an experience of early learning?

2. What sorts of opportunities to connect with and notice children on a deep level are available here?

Just after 8:00 a.m. the children begin to arrive. Upon arrival they are expected to put away their backpacks and make their way to an easel upon which is written the morning check-in —a question or action that invites the child to make some sort of mark on the board. If the children finish early, they are invited to write in their journals or read books. At 8:20 their teacher reminds them that morning meeting is soon, and they begin meeting with a greeting—but not until everyone is seated. Meeting must be done by 8:45 so that the children can head to an enrichment course that will last for 30 minutes.

Just after 8:00 a.m. the children begin to arrive. Upon arrival they are expected to put away their backpacks. After putting away their backpacks, the children are free to move about the classroom. On various tables, the teachers have arranged materials—for creating art; building with small blocks; and making stories using small dolls, bolts of fabric, and open-ended recycled parts. At 8:20 the teacher singsongs a reminder that a class meeting will begin in five minutes, and by 8:25 most of the children are seated on the meeting rug. One teacher begins the meeting with a welcome chant, and, as he does, the other children make their way over. Although they would like to be finished by 8:45, their next planned activity isn't until 9:30, leaving time for flexibility.

These vignettes each incorporate elements of morning arrival practices that have been part of my experiences in the classroom. My goal is not necessarily to paint one as better than the other (although there is definitely one that most appeals to my sensibilities). Rather, note the ways that each classroom constitutes a unique context in which children will spend their days. Each of these contexts makes its own assumptions about what a child needs, what is best for them, and what sorts of rituals and activities should have priority in their days. In doing so, it reveals an image of children.

Consideration 3: What Has Your Formation Looked Like?

Our images of children and childhood are also influenced by the formation we receive as educators. A quick look at the missions, goals, and outcomes of various early childhood programs reveals that they approach children and childhood from different perspectives. Of course all are focused generally on working with and caring for young children, but they conceptualize their goals differently.

My alma mater, the Erikson Institute, describes itself on its website as dedicated to building "knowledge in the service of children," and considers itself as striving "to educate, inspire, and promote leadership that supports children and their families in reaching their fullest potential." According to its website, the Bank Street College of Education writes that they "see in education the opportunity to build a better society" and that "social justice, advocacy, and building an inclusive community are at the core of our work." Another program website describes itself as having "a heavy emphasis on professional growth [with] multiple opportunities for résumé development" (Louisiana State University), and still another insists that they wish their coursework to be "as practical as possible," where "the goal for each course will be to have each student generate a product that is tangibly useful in their work situation" (Antioch University of New England).

It is not surprising, then, that a first-year teacher coming from any of these teacher preparation programs would have a different understanding of children, their needs, their abilities, and how to best serve them.

The downstream effects of these differential trajectories of formation, perhaps, are more familiar topics of discussion for educators, as they influence the very core of the ways that we engage with, interact with, and provide for the children in our care. For example, what are your thoughts on how one might balance children's need for play with the intentional exposure to early academic skills and dispositions necessary for them to navigate later years of schooling? What do you think of the role of the materials and the environment in children's creativity, agency, and inquiry? Does watching a child climbing a tall tree sound exciting or terrifying? Should conversations around children's rough-and-tumble play be grounded in the children's interpretations of their experiences, or is it more important to consider the thoughts of families, parents, and regulatory bodies? While there is, perhaps, no single right answer to any of these questions, the point is that the educational formation of each teacher is highly dependent on where they learn about teaching and childhood. What's more is that the above examples are only the differences in the articulated missions of early childhood teacher preparation programs and, as such, can only capture a sliver of the extreme variance experienced in individual centers and classrooms. When you add the additional consideration of coteachers, budgets, communities, and the compositions of children in classrooms, it becomes evident that one's image of the child is impossibly nuanced. And not only that, it is also flexible.

Constructing Our Own Image of the Child

Our image of children, then, is the result of multilayered intersecting processes of our own experiences as children, of our formation as educators and practitioners, and of the everyday experiences we have with children. As you read the following story from my time at NOLA Nature School in New Orleans, I invite you to see whether you can identify some of the instances in which I, as the teacher, might be gathering information and experiences that contribute to my image of the child.

It is a rainy day and puddles surround a large oak tree. A group of three-, four-, and five-year-olds in brightly colored rainsuits splash with abandon, their voices rising above the pelting roar of the deluge. It is a cycle of splashing, laughter, and gleeful falling. They continue like this for nearly twenty minutes until their teachers decide to move to a new, drier location for snacktime.

Louis and I are seated on the playground on a warm day. We are both somewhat subdued, watching with half interest as his classmates play nearby. It is one of those days where everything feels slower, more pensive. After some time, Louis turns to me and asks, "Mr. Ron, what do you think about clouds? Like, how are they up there?"

The children have been playing war for many days in a row. After reading a book where the children set up their own society, Leo exclaims, "We're being in the book! Let me check it to see what we can do!" At this he flips the page back to the page that features the war.

"Have you heard of the big hungry T-Rex who eats trees, eats water bottles to get the water he needs?" Louis asks the group. "But dinosaurs don't climb trees," Rosemary asserts. "I said eat," Louis reiterates. Kyle chimes in, "But I been watching Dino Pups and the orange T-Rex." "But what does your mom say?" Leo asks. "My mom just says we can watch Dino Pups, and it has a T-Rex in it," comes Kyle's matter-of-fact reply.

In observing children (as they splash in the rain), in talking with children (as we sit on the playground), in reading and working with children (as we encounter a new story together), and through listening to children (as we eat lunch together), I form a picture of what it means to be a child. One might consider each piece of our work with children, every child we encounter, every piece of media we consume that references children, to be a pixel or a brushstroke. Singly, it tells us very little, but when a great number of brushstrokes or pixels appear together, the result is a fuller picture—an image.

Therefore, in addition to our experiences as children and what we have learned from others about children, we form images of children through our daily lives with them that are inexhaustibly rich.

WHY OUR IMAGE OF THE CHILD IS IMPORTANT

The purpose of this chapter so far has been to emphasize that as educators, we already have an "image of the child," whether we realize it or not. I hope that you have been invited and challenged to name your own, to deconstruct and then reassemble it into a form approaching intelligibility. The reason this has merited such a close consideration is that the entire purpose of this book is, at its core, to invite us to reform our image of the child. But before we can reform something— or even understand it as worthy *of* reform—it is in our interest to elaborate why. As mentioned throughout this chapter, our image of the child informs absolutely everything about our work with and for young children.

✦✦ **Our images of childhood influence the interactions we have with children.**
The ways that we approach and interact with children, how we speak to them, support them, or console them, are based on and influenced by our image of children and childhood. Of course the image of the child of any individual person is also in conversation with the aforementioned (societal, cultural, institutional) images of children, but all of these find their point of impact at the level of educator interaction.

✦✦ **Our images of children and childhood determine the opportunities we afford children in classroom and care spaces.**
The opportunities we afford children are also based on our images of children and childhood. Do children deserve opportunities to get messy? Should they be able to engage in a risky behavior that lies at the cusp of our adult level of comfort? Our responses, as well, are evidence of our images of children and childhood—consolation, encouragement, and so on. In many early childhood contexts, the discontinuity in images of the child is evident to children. Children know who to ask to climb up the slide the wrong way and who not to ask. They know who to ask for an extra snack, with whom they prefer to engage in a teacher-led activity—all of these are multilayered decisions, sure. However, at some level, all involve a child's implicit understanding of an educator's image of them.

✦✦ **Our images of children and childhood influence the images that families and other systems of care are forming of children.**
As educators, we are (at least in ideal circumstances) trusted individuals in the life of the family system of which the child is an important member. This trust, combined with the inherent authority that comes with spending the majority of

a child's waking hours with them, means that we have significant impact on the ways that children view their experiences in contexts of early care and on how their families understand this as well. As a result of our influence in the lives of families, our ideas about children and the ways we share these influence the community at large. How, for example, are we communicating with families about their children? How do we frame difficult moments of the day? How do we interpret and translate moments for families, to support them in coming to understand their children on new and deeper levels?

✦✦ Our images of children influence the questions we can ask about childhood itself.

Our images of the child even inform the questions we ask and wonder about childhood. If we understand children as complex, we will ask complex questions about children. If we believe children are creative, we will wonder at the depths of their creativity and consider how we might extend and support it. If we believe children need freedom to explore, we will ask ourselves and our colleagues how we facilitate an environment where exploration is possible.

✦✦ Our images of children and childhood influence the ways that children see themselves.

As adults in children's lives, all of these realities converge in an extremely important point—that the way we see children and, via that image, the interactions that we have with children, contribute to their images of self. These images of self (also referred to as *self-concept*) have wide-ranging and long-lasting effects on children's well-being, their measures of belongingness and connectedness within school spaces, and even on their various measures of cognitive performance (Ladd 1990).

IN CLOSING: CHILDREN AND CHILDHOOD IN CONVERSATION

As educators, our relationships with and orientations toward children are unique. When it comes to any given child, we are some of the only people in the world who do or will ever know this child on such a deep level at this vulnerable, fascinating, creative time in their life. In fact, when it comes to how a child is at school, as a social actor in a community of peers and friends, no other adult knows (or at least has the potential to know) that child as well as the educators who are working in the classroom with them. Our responsibility, then, is significant. We are tasked with showing sides of children that others do not have access to and cannot know or see—our insights into children and their experiences may affirm, challenge, or completely upend and surprise those who know them well. One way I like to think about this often is that as educators, we are reintroducing a child to their community of care when we share about their days and their lives as lived in schools and spaces of care.

In addition to reintroducing a child to their caregiving community, we also reintroduce children to themselves. As educators, we celebrate children, showing them who they are when they are engaged with peers in the school context—a context created, at least primarily, for their development and thriving.

All said, what this boils down to is that each moment of a child's life as they are living it in the space they share with us—and how we translate and share those moments—matters.

As educators in the modern era, we must acknowledge that every aspect of our current profession is situated, which is another way of saying that the work we do is in conversation with centuries of ideas, movements, and social and cultural shifts, as well as with contemporary societal, institutional, and cultural influences—all of which has led us to this particular moment in time. We are, at the same time, operating within spaces that are highly unique, with children who both individually and collectively contribute to a classroom culture that has never existed before and will never exist again.

Therefore, as we begin to formulate our images of children, to reimage and reconstruct them, it is important that we do so with the awareness that every moment, every day, is filled with significance.

Reflections

What words, phrases, and ideas come to mind when you reflect on your image of children?

Where have your images of children and childhood been formed?

How did the adults in your life view children when you were a child? What elements of these patterns of thinking do you still hold? What aspects of your current thinking have shifted?

How, in your day-to-day work with children, do you concretize components of this image?

Are there any images of children and/or childhood that you resist? Why?

Chapter 2
The Inexhaustible
Richness of the Day

INTRODUCTION: FRAMING THE WHAT, WHY, AND HOW OF INEXHAUSTIBLE RICHNESS

It is true, almost by definition, that ordinary moments fill most of the child's day. . . . At the end of the day the ordinary moments constitute the child's story (Forman, Hall, and Berglund 2001, 52).

Being able to see the ways that our days, spent in the joy and thrall of working with and living alongside young children, are filled with meaning is a critical piece of working in the field of early childhood. Yes, there are big moments that deserve to be celebrated and marked, but everything from the walk to the playground to the asides children make as they wait in line for a turn at the slide is a moment that merits wonder. Each moment, however small and seemingly insignificant, tells us something about a child specifically and, perhaps, about childhood more broadly as *well. Where, in your own days, do you already experience rich, meaningful moments? Where, with a little reflection, might you find many more?*

The central focus of this chapter is how, through reconsidering the everyday moments that take place in our work with children, we can come to see—and in seeing, be able to share—more and more of the depth of what children are doing in moments that are viewed as otherwise unremarkable or routine. We begin by reflecting on the satisfaction that can accrue to us when we begin to view the mundane as meaningful, and then build on this thinking by exploring how this view aligns with children's own views of their lives. Next, we explore how the use of intentional language, the honing of our eyes, and the act of writing ourselves into the narratives that unfold each day all contribute to a new way of thinking about, speaking about, and engaging with children and the work we do with them.

LOCATING WONDER

For children there is wonder everywhere. Under a rock, up a tree, in the hum of a busy bee, the flight of birds, a lawn mower buzzing, clipping, and cutting. Meaningful moments occur at every instant of the day.

What if I were to invite you to imagine a rich moment from your day with young children? What is unfolding? Are you, perhaps, in the classroom, engaged in a small-group exploration? Are you at circle time, where something has caught the ears of all gathered? Is the moment entirely child-led, such as one child narrating the ideal technique as another strives to climb a tall tree, or a group of children having a lively discussion about what it means to be alive or dead? Or was it the walk that your class took from one space to another, pausing along the way to look at a flower in bloom from a crack in the concrete?

Jon: Do you wanna play tag?

Jon tags William, who is sitting down. William does not respond.

Jon: I said, "Do you wanna play tag?"

William: No, I wanna play, but I don't wanna play tag.

Jon: Okay, what do you wanna play? (Pauses.) This is the single game.

His mind, it seems, has changed.

William sits in reply. Silently.

Jon (with greater emphasis): This is the single game, tag.

William (relentingly): Okay.

William grabs a stick he had used for an earlier game and prepares to bolt.

Jon (shouting): No sticks! No sticks in this game!

This is a typical moment in early childhood friendships, right? You might see nothing particularly special here. After all, one child wants to play with another who only wants to play a certain game. There is a back-and-forth between the two children as each is hesitant to relent. However, with time, the desire to play supersedes the desire to play a specific thing, and the children move past their momentary disagreement and begin playing a game that, ultimately, both enjoy.

However, that is not the only story here. There is more richness than immediately meets the eye.

What if we knew that Jon was experimenting with what it meant to be a leader and that William, typically the leader, worked hard to push past his own desire to play Lava Monster in order to play with his dear friend? How might that change this "unremarkable" moment?

We could also consider what it meant that William was willing to convey his emotions to Jon and make note of Jon's question to William, "What do you wanna to play?" We begin to see evidence of empathy, respect, and independent perspective-taking—Jon asks, William feels safe enough to share, and Jon is secure enough (in either authority or friendship or both) to reassert his own desire.

This moment is anything but unremarkable—and the truth is that nearly every moment of a child's day is like this.

RECONCEPTUALIZING RICHNESS AND MEANING

We often think of rich moments as those that feel "special" for some reason. We think about the things that occur that are perhaps out of the normal, those that leave us with a feeling of warmth and satisfaction (never mind that these subjective emotions are elicited by experiences that are highly variable and dependent on a variety of individual and contextual features). In a way, this is also evidence that we view "richness" as something held in moments that fulfill our own ends, goals, and ideas about what early childhood needs to look like. For example, describing children's engagement in a small group as rich may be valid, but if we are *only* viewing as rich those children's activities that look like the learning we expect or have been trained to see, we are missing many points of entry. **Mundane moments are meaningful.** If we don't reframe the mundane as rich, we are, by implication, suggesting that a child's day holds little for us to be interested in—which is, at least according to the image of the child developed in the previous chapter, wholly untrue. We are forever and ever resisting the oversimplification.

Imagine:

It is just after ten o'clock in the morning. You are seated at your kitchen table, and a diffuse light streams in from a window out of which you can see your front lawn, garden, and porch. You are sipping a cup of coffee and go to pick up the book you've been reading, but not before checking your phone and noticing a text from a friend. You exchange a few messages and then, remembering your original intention, pick up the book you have been making your way through for some time. You sip, sit, and read for thirty minutes before going out to your garden to tend to the plants before continuing on with the rest of your day.

Now, imagine this:

It is just after ten o'clock in the morning. You are seated at snack, and a diffuse light streams in from a window out of which you see the bean sprouts your class planted the week before. You are sipping a cup of water, holding it shakily in your hands—but not dropping it! You look over at the blocks and start to walk there—but then you remember you are sitting next to your favorite friend. You choose to talk to them instead, and for the next twenty minutes you talk, eat, and drink before getting up, washing your hands, and going outside to look at the bean sprouts together.

Are these moments merely mundane? Are they rich with information, meaning, and value? The answer to both questions is "Yes!" These moments are about nothing, and at the same time they are about everything that is important. There is an everything-ness even to the moments that appear as nothing-full.

Think about your experience at the table. How your coffee tastes, how delightful it might feel to see your garden, the fruit of your labor and trial-and-error growing. How nice it feels to connect with a friend, and how that connection is so meaningful and valuable that you defer your original intention. How the reading that takes place after is sweet, unhurried, and gives you food for thought that you'll meditate on for the next day or two or more. How a quick check-in with your garden, a little song you sing to the growing plants, all are evidence of your internal state and prepare you for continued action in the world while simultaneously constituting a grounding force for you.

To describe this chunk of time in your day as meaningless or purely one long transition is not only false but also does a disservice to the great intention you bring to it. Is it now evident, then, that to do similarly with children would be to miss out on so much? Mundane is never meaningless.

All of this said, the inexhaustible richness is not something that has been lost on education entirely. On the contrary, the work of many researchers, educators, and educational researchers speaks to the fullness of the most ostensibly mundane moments of children's days. In doing so, they revealed a few things:

First, that this perspective makes our work with children exciting and stimulating.

Second, that (as many educators have likely long inferred) children view these moments as important!

I also want to suggest that, third, this view helps us develop a new lexicon—a new way of speaking—about children and childhood.

THE MEANINGFUL MUNDANE MAKES OUR WORK SATISFYING

For many of us, watching children play is both interesting and, at the same time, utterly unremarkable for its ordinariness. Play is frequent and occurs whether or not we are trying to facilitate it (and even despite the efforts of some to curtail it). Play is mundane and unremarkable and, at the same time, gives insight into experiences that are full of nuance and meaning.

In her book *Really Seeing Children*, Deb Curtis (2017, 13) writes that, in children's earliest years, "there are no ordinary moments," emphasizing that underneath the surface of everything that is unfolding in a child's day there is a parallel, connected process that yields an insight into what is happening. Curtis goes on to devote an entire book to helping educators see the processes of learning and development that are unfolding even in the most ostensibly mundane moments. A similar book, *The Art of Awareness*, explicitly invites educators into a deep presence in every moment of their time with children. In this volume, Curtis and coauthor Margie Carter (2022) invite us, again, to notice, document, and illuminate children's everyday moments as if they were "medieval manuscripts" whose meanings are made increasingly visible and accessible through rigorous documentation (see chapter 12 of *The Art of Awareness* for Curtis and Carter's more extended reflections on this issue).

The Diary of Laura by Carolyn Edwards and Carlina Rinaldi (2008) is a striking example of what is possible when educators adopt a perspective that appreciates the richness of everyday moments. Educators come to look at moments such as diapering as full of value and import.

In my own work, this reality has been repeatedly underscored. But more on Wanders (a long hike where the wandering is the goal) and walks later! For now, let it suffice to say that adopting a rich perspective means that the daily, little, tiny moments—otherwise unseen—become exciting and intriguing sources of information. Even when we are tired, even when we feel overwhelmed, even when there is so much—too much—we remain curious, invigorated, and even amazed.

However, if we stopped here, we would fail. After all, our own motivations and interests, however valuable, are not the central reason we ought to respect children's lives. The single most important reason we ought to regard the mundane moments as valuable, important, exciting—as rich—is because that is how children themselves see them.

CHILDREN VIEW EVERYDAY MOMENTS AS SIGNIFICANT

Research and theory align with what is, at least for many of us, likely in line with personal experience, that the everyday moments of children's lives are not only meaningful in some high-level adult-centered sense but that children, too, see immense value within their daily lives.

Research by Stephanie Serriere (2010) used photographs to explore children's perceptions of everyday moments. Her research, though explicitly focused on the ways that child-centered curricula could promote democratic practices through documenting and discussing children's play, also reveals the depth of everyday experiences as interpreted by children. Over the course of three years, Serriere took photographs of children in play or open-ended exploration in early childhood classrooms. She then used these photographs to stimulate discussions with children about their lives, experiences, and relationships during whole-group, small-group, and one-on-one meetings. Children's commentaries touched on a variety of themes including, among other things, fairness, the ideal classroom, and children's ideal selves. These ordinary moments, the everyday instances of play, exploration, and interaction, were the moments from which children were beginning to construct their understanding of big ideas.

A seminal study by Icelandic scholar Johanna Einarsdottir (2005) invited preschoolers to take pictures of the things that were important to them in their preschool. Children's photographs ultimately included everything from activity boards and other children to outdoor play spaces, private spaces, and hallways. Ultimately, each of these studies serves to remind us that when children are asked either to capture or comment, the ostensibly mundane features of their daily lives are the ones that stand out as the most notable.

Indeed, when one considers literature written about children and child development, the potency of mundane moments is doubly confirmed. Developmental research reveals that everything from the pragmatics of language to which emotions are appropriate to display and when; what toys one ought to play with; and attitudes about gender, race, goodness, and more are all conveyed through everyday actions that, on the surface, appear to be of little note.

Sociological and anthropological theory and research also affirm that mundane actions and rituals constitute mechanisms through which children intuit and learn societal norms and social mores. William Corsaro (2015, 19) writes that "the habitual, taken-for-granted character of [cultural] routines provides children . . . security and shared understanding of belonging to a social group." These routines, originally introduced by parents, are quickly reproduced by young children in their own social groupings through play. This *interpretive reproduction* (Corsaro 2015) occurs, significantly, in children's play.

Indeed, play is the quintessential example of a series of moments, rituals, and interactions that is simultaneously mundane and impossibly rich and nuanced. While play is often defined as a self-chosen, child-directed activity that is guided by flexible rules, understood to be unreal, and during which a child is alert and unstressed (Gray 2013), it's likely that we have all seen play that at least begins to trouble the neat boundaries of this definition. However, what is less up for debate is that in play children meld everyday words, actions, and dispositions in a fantasy world of endless potential. Social issues surrounding race, gender, ability, access, violence, trauma, and death are all part of the conversation as children engage in this everyday activity. Vivian Paley (2004) and Jane Katch (2003), among many others, expertly chronicle this intersection. The deep realities of life are worked out in the little, often invisible or overlooked, yet extraordinarily rich moments of the everyday:

A group of children play with sticks. In a nature-based preschool where we spend days outside, this is among the most common occurrences. I take a photo nonetheless; one of the many I happen to take on any given day.

I print out the photo along with some others some days later and bring them to our morning meeting, choosing one to place in the floorbook. I ask the children, "What was your favorite part about this game?"

"I like that I can throw sticks really far."

"Why is stick fighting so fun?" I wonder aloud.

"Because you get to knock sticks out of hands."

"Trey tried to get us."

Just here, a game of stick play is seen to have multiple layers. The games are social, they are competitive, they have opportunities to see how far and how high one can throw. They are opportunities to push and test boundaries, to understand one's own as, for example, when William suggests a firm rule.

"No pushing down," William says. As he speaks, he points to a photo: "That [photo shows] the pushing." A game of stick play is also, furthermore, an opportunity to consider how the aims of a collective enterprise (the game) make certain behaviors off-limits. "Do not throw sticks into the water, because that is not a point of your game," Louis offers.

And regardless of whether we agree with Louis or William about the rules of engagement they propose or the purposes they ascribe to their and their peers' play, we can see, even in these smallest snippets of their own reflection on their actions, how nuanced children's play—how nuanced children's everyday interactions—can be.

A NEW WAY OF SPEAKING: CHILDREN'S COMPLEXITIES

While the diverse literatures on children's lives and the richness that can be found there are often speaking to broader themes—such as emergent literacy or numeracy or social and emotional development—each confirms for us the critical nature of the everyday. Those small, so-visible-they're-invisible actions are crucial in shaping our experiences of many of the things that end up having the greatest impacts on our lived experiences in the world.

However, I want to wonder, briefly, what we can learn from children's small moments that extends outside of typical ways of speaking about children. These moments, too, carry valuable significance, like the following exchange between William and Leo that reveals two children thinking about and wrestling with their impacts on the natural world.

We are gathered together in an open field when the children notice a heron alighting a few dozen feet away. Louis chases the heron, and it flies away but only a few meters. Malcolm, arms out, runs toward it, yelling, "Fly, bird! Fly!" The heron, as if not needing to be told more than once, flies farther away. The cycle repeats four more times. A child chases—the heron flies. A child chases—the heron flies. A child chases—the heron flies. Finally, the heron flies away.

A significant part of our time at the NOLA Nature School involves inviting the children into a consideration of the way we human beings relate to the other denizens of the natural world. Therefore, my coteacher Abby's open-ended musing is not out of place.

Abby: Six times, I noticed, that heron flew away.

Leo: Because the kids were chasing the bird. (A brief pause.) It's [saying,] "Leave me alone!"

William's matter-of-fact tone conveys his more literal perspective: I can't hear it talk. Animals only talk in shows.

Leo (with a hint of exasperation): It says it inside its body.

This conversation, or more accurately, the few lines of it that were captured, reveal a great deal about what the children think and where their meanings are still being worked out while spanning the disciplines of biology, philosophy, and critical media studies. Biologically the children are curious: How do animals communicate? Philosophically, they wonder: What does it mean to be a human in a world where other animals are fearful of us? What do we do with this? Critical media perspectives wonder: How are the animals we encounter in the fictional world of television, of the popular media, different than those we encounter up close and personally in real life? Power, responsibility, identity—all within a few lines.

DEVELOPING AN EYE FOR THE OVERLOOKED

Developing an eye for the invisible means that we have to (1) look everywhere; (2) describe the small details; and (3) be willing to tell the same story many, many times. Looking everywhere is the result of developing a curious disposition about children's lives in the world.

When we come to see that these everyday moments are filled with endless possibility and significance, we are left to wonder: How do we respond? What is a concrete way to honor this richness? How do we develop our eye for the unseen features and perspectives of life that we now know and agree are present?

Look Everywhere

Overall, in an echo of and in conversation with the work of Deb Curtis (2017, 8), I want to invite us into a teaching practice that, as she writes, "notice[s] and suspend[s] adult agendas." Adult agendas such as the documentation of learning goals and progress toward developmental milestones, state and national frameworks, and center-specific goals are not bad. They are necessary components of our work as early educators and, in justice to the children with whom we work, we are obligated to make connections between their daily doings and these agendas. However, what Curtis is implying, and I am striving to make explicit, is that we cannot stop here.

Let us consider the children's trip to the Spooky House:

On February 3, 2022, our class took a walk from our school building around the corner to a house the children called the "Spooky House." The Spooky House was a large purple house with signs out front that read everything from "Go your own way" to "Wi-Fi hotspot," and even one with a picture of a velociraptor that read "Electrified fence." A tarp covered the front door. Whatever our adult minds might have intuited about the set of circumstances influencing the visual condition of the house (such as a resident with a flair for the whimsical or who left their Halloween decorations up a few months beyond October), the children were fascinated by it, lingering for upward of ten minutes to gaze at the facade of the house whenever we would walk by (which they also wanted to do quite often).

So, one day we walked to the Spooky House. On the way, the children played, and when we got to the house the children spent time looking at and wondering about the house. After a few minutes, we returned to school just in time for lunch.

This is a simple story. It tells us about a group of children who walked from their school to a place in their neighborhood and then walked back to their school in time for lunch. This is an example of a story where we might look for more. What, really, is here?

Although the vignette as it is written above is an accurate description of an event that actually took place, it captures only a small piece of a series of rich occurrences that took place. The vignette above centers the children's experiences at the house itself and frames the walks to and from the house merely as transitional.

While these walks indeed *were* transitions, what might a closer look, a look that views this as inexhaustibly rich, reveal?

Describe the Small Details

The fact remains that whatever our obligations to children as fellow humans, whatever the extent of our inclinations toward anthropological and sociological stances in our interactions with and thinking about them, we are also educators—a role that, in our society, comes with certain obligations. One of those obligations is to document children's lives: the play, creativity, learning, development, and inquiry that takes place each day. Of course documentation can look many ways—it can be a picture, a video, a note scrawled on a sheet of paper, a narrative typed up and sent home, and much more—but at its core it is an indication of regard for a child's experience. Understanding that each day is inexhaustibly rich means that we document the mundane experiences alongside those that, for whatever reason, stick out to us as significant.

Documenting every moment is impossible. Yet documenting small moments, even with a simple written note or a snapped picture, is much more possible. I also want to contend that doing so does at least three things:

First, it sensitizes us to the richness of a child's day.

Second, it illuminates previously unseen or unnoticed threads and connections.

Third, it begins to shift our perceptions (and those of our colleagues) of what moments merit documentation.

Here's an example: Documenting the mundane along the way to the Spooky House opened up even more of the depth of the walk. Consider these descriptions of photographs taken from the walk to the house.

11:18 a.m. Four children sit around an open journal. Cara looks at the house numbers in front of her. Kyle, hands out, looks down.

11:19 a.m. Cara and Luke are now walking, hand in hand, down the street. Luke is saying something to Cara, who resolutely looks ahead.

11:19 a.m. Griff, holding his journal, peers through the ventilation grate of a house through which he can see, faintly, light streaming through the grate to the other end of the crawl space.

11:20 a.m. Griff and Cara are kneeling over their journals. Cara looks up at Laura with a smile on her face—mid-laugh, perhaps.

11:21 a.m. Griff jumps from one cement path to the other, one arm outstretched in front of him, the other holding his journal close to his body.

11:21 a.m. Kyle jumps from one side to the other also. His tongue is sticking out—he is focused. Griff watches from where he landed.

11:23 a.m. A series of photos shows Griff and Kyle making this into a game.

11:24 a.m. Luke holds a clump of mud and brings it close to his face.

11:25 a.m. A video still shows Griff and Kyle running and falling on the grass between street and sidewalk.

We have made a chronicle of a series of deeply meaningful experiences that occurred between our departure from school at 11:17 a.m. and our arrival at the Spooky House at 11:26 a.m. Within the space of nine minutes, a multitude of stories unfolded that would have been obscured or even erased by a failure to look closely at these *moments-in-between*.

Even if you don't have the tools or capacity to document every instance, it can be helpful to begin by opening yourself up to the small ways stories are unfolding in the moments of your everyday goings-on. What stories might you notice the next time you find yourself with a group of children?

Tell the Same Story Anew Each Time

Ultimately, interpreting the day as full of inexhaustible richness means that we are invited, challenged even, to embrace each day with a disposition of curiosity. Instead of viewing our days as hours filled with boxes to check, we can view them as opportunities to be continually surprised, impressed, wowed, and astounded in the most wonderful ways at the life we are experiencing alongside other humans.

Think about a relationship you value. This relationship may be with a dear friend, a romantic partner, a family member, or a loved one. When you meet up with this person, do your actions follow a predictable routine? Do you always, for example, go for a walk in the park with your partner before dinner? Does the fact that you do it every day mean that it is not important or special? Is every walk the same, or are there some days when the same action in the same place at the same time takes on an entirely different meaning depending on contextual features, such as the weather, what the day has been like, what is occurring around you, or what have you?

Now, imagine a child, ideally one (or a group of them) with whom you work. It is likely that they enter the same classroom each day—or at least rotate between familiar environments on a regular basis. It is also likely that they encounter many, if not all, of the same children most days—their friends, colleagues, and loved ones in their school community. This mundanity does not diminish the meaning of these daily occurrences, and one might even argue the mundanity is what enables the meaning these moments take on to deepen.

Let us now tell the story of another walk to the Spooky House:

> For us, these wandering walks were common occurrences, taking place multiple times a week. However, rather than write them off as just another thing we did, my coteacher and I consistently reminded ourselves that there were forever interesting and valuable stories happening even within the bounds of regularity.
>
> On this day, the children took their journals with them. Cara, who loved writing, was the first to opt in to carrying her journal with her. Her peers were quickly inspired to bring theirs as well. And so we walked to the Spooky House, me stretching my legs and the children holding journals, together. It was a walk we had taken before and a walk we would take again in the future. And yet it was still special.

Just because something has happened before does not mean that we know everything there is to know about it or that we have or can discern every ounce of meaning it holds in the life of an individual and/or community.

CAPTURING THE RICHNESS OF THE DAYS

In this final section of the chapter, I felt it was important to put a few notes here that didn't fit neatly into the other sections of the chapter. Just because something doesn't fit neatly into a box we've made doesn't mean it is any less important. Here I explore a little about what it means to write oneself in and to consider richness from a child's perspective.

Writing Ourselves In

I invite us to imagine a world in which early childhood educators take cues from their colleagues in sociology and anthropology and write themselves in. The idea of writing oneself into a piece of research refers to seeing the influence and impact of one's ideas, perspectives, and agendas on the ways that one interprets what occurs within a context. Interpreting the significance of a child's day and life through an adult lens fails to write the adult in, and without this initial writing in it is impossible to write oneself back out. Only by seeing the agendas that we typically have and the power we wield can we begin to set aside spaces and times, however small, where we actively counteract and work against these tendencies to unduly influence contexts. Let us return to the case of the Spooky House.

A simplistic description might say something like this:

On Friday, the children decided to go for a walk to the Spooky House.

Writing myself in might look something like this:

On 2/3, I asked the children if they would like to go on a Wander. Five of them said yes, they would, and at 11:17 a.m. our journey began. I set out with the intention to take this walk slowly, wanting to stretch my own legs for a bit as well.

This reveals my own agency and allows me and others to be able to see how my goals as the adult—to get out—might have made room for what occurs later on. It pushes against a simplified narrative of children deciding to do something and extends and enriches it by showing how even the most basic decisions are a complex dance of desires (to go for a walk, to see the Spooky House, to stretch one's legs) that enter into lively and productive conversation.

When we write ourselves "in" in order to write ourselves back "out," we begin to hone a disposition that displaces the teacher as an authority. In the second example above, my intentions are simply to get moving and stretch my legs. I have made myself, my honest self, visible. I have also emphasized that the children did not simply "decide" to go for a walk, but they responded to my bid to go on a walk—and, what's more, not all of them said yes. Each of these small additions are included so that when others encounter this narrative, they will have a better understanding of the ways that my own and the children's intentions intersect on the way to an experience that, all said, ended up being magical. These small occasional glimpses into the reality show that, far from being an absolute authority, educators and adults are (older) people in conversation with (younger) people. When we are, however briefly, on the same level with children, we are able to be curious in a way that lets us see and escape the metaphorical box where we keep our typical ways of speaking about our daily actions and interactions with children.

Our Views versus Children's Views

I believe that when we have regard for the moments of a child's life only insofar as they fit into a predefined framework, it is no regard at all. If we try to define value for children through an adult lens, we are using what is referred to as an "etic" approach—to take what one observes within a particular group of individuals who are part of a different culture and to interpret those actions and their assumed ends/goals as if they were part of one's own culture. Let us imagine, for example, a photo of two young children holding hands. There are many possible interpretations, and if we used an etic approach in which we interpreted this gesture merely in terms of a particular framework of children's development, we might classify this mundane action as an indication of friendship between two children. We might even go as far as to say that it isn't really important at all. While either of these inferences might be correct, they do not fully account for the possibilities.

An "emic" approach to interpreting this gesture would, instead, consider the children's culture—their experiences, ways of being, and practices as they see and experience them—in evaluating what this hand-holding means. Think for a moment: When do children hold hands? For young children, hand-holding is a gesture that adults use to keep them safe, often when crossing streets, entering busy public spaces, or when they are at risk of endangering themselves. Adults also are likely to hold children's hands when a child is feeling afraid. Perhaps, then, the hand-holding we have observed signals that a child is concerned with a peer's safety or seeking reassurance in an uncertain or fearful situation. Further, this gesture of hand-holding for safety, for a child at least, is something that a teacher or adult who is responsible for them may do regardless of how much or little affection is felt. Therefore, to conclude it is a gesture of friendship and to use it as an example of such (lacking other context) might be a mischaracterization of the child's intention.

Part of embracing the concept of inexhaustible richness involves acknowledging the reality that our interpretations may fall short of the mark and cannot and never will be able to capture the complexity of everything we experience.

A FINAL WORD

Each time we dive deeply into the richness of the days children are living, we are reminding ourselves and others that children are *living* at school. At school, children are learning skills, making connections between domains of academic, social, and emotional learning—but, what's more, they are forming ideas about themselves and the world and musing about their understandings of the world as filtered through media, and they are making bodies of artistic work and judging the merits of their own and others' endeavors. The value of what happens in children's lives at school extends far beyond the accessible boxes or categories that adults, however well-meaning, fit them into. I am attempting to emphasize again how important it is to reframe our priorities surrounding what happens in the school day—to choose where we direct our attention. We are reinforcing for children that the moments they experience in school, even the small ones, matter. We are also venturing into a new territory—one that takes us beyond the province of children and families and into conversation with the early childhood context where we find ourselves. As educators, we have a direct impact on the discourses and conversations that families in our centers are engaging in. What we emphasize in our documentation communicates not only what we think about children but also what we, figures of developmental and educational authority, view as valuable knowledge. When we make a big deal of small moments and small stories from the day, we are advocating for what matters.

Working with young children is intense, exciting, exhausting, and extraordinarily worthwhile. Our days are filled with what can at times feel like endless monotony—play, gathering, snacktime, outside time, small groups, diapering, potty breaks, lunch, nap, play, repeat. Occasionally, something novel occurs, leaving us surprised and (depending on what exactly the "something" is) fearful, intrigued, curious, or otherwise wondering. This is the reality of our work.

However, by honing an appreciation for those mundanities that make up the majority of our cycles of daily living with young children, we can begin to see how no matter what, our days are filled with information. We are not only watching as children live. We are not only living alongside children. We are also building on, extending, revising, interrogating, and reimagining images of the child that lay at the intersections of multiple disciplines.

And we, those who work with and care for young children, are better positioned than anyone else to do this work.

Reflections

What are the places in your day where you are already seeing richness? What other layers might you be missing?

Might you challenge yourself to take an otherwise typical, unremarkable-seeming moment and illuminate it more in-depth?

Ask the children what their favorite moments of the day are. What do they say? Why might they be saying that, and what can you learn from their sharing?

If you like, experiment with writing yourself in to an existing narrative that only features the children. What were you thinking, why did you choose to capture this moment, and what did you do before and/or in response?

How might you reframe your conversations with colleagues, caregivers, and others to increasingly emphasize the mundane moments?

~ Chapter 3 ~

Uniquely Proximate Positioning

INTRODUCTION: LOOKING AT CHILDREN'S LIVES UP CLOSE

One of the most difficult things about teaching preschool, at least in my own experience, is that you are constantly on. We have to be closely attending to and, more often than not, physically close to the children in our care. In this chapter, we discuss the uniquely proximate positioning of the educator. What are the implications of the reality that, as early childhood educators, we spend our days immersed in children's worlds, concerns, play, ideas, speech, and (less joyfully and sometimes hilariously) fluids? Over the course of our time in this chapter, we consider the fact that within school spaces, we know children better than anyone else. Not even parents understand a child within a group of peers at school in the ways we as educators do. What, this chapter wonders, do we do with this?

In the first part of this chapter, we explore some concrete moments of proximity, considering the dimensions along which educators know children better than any other adult. We also discuss how the obligations of being an educator enable us to have this knowledge and emphasize that it is a complementary (not necessarily superior or inferior) knowledge to that of parents and other caregivers. Next, we digress briefly to unpack notions of authenticity, asking who, if anyone, can assert that they have access to children's authentic voices or experiences. Finally, we explore some of what this proximity enables us to do, to see, and to know about the lives and experiences of the children in our care.

~

PROXIMITY TO CHILDREN

Eye to eye, nose to nose, face-to-face, snuggled-up and held, singing songs, holding hands, dressing wounds, listening, soothing, laughing, learning and teaching, collaborating and wondering—relationship.

As early childhood educators, most of our days are spent being with young children and thinking about young children. We observe young children as they bid farewell to their families, as they connect with friends. We know what they are like at their best and at their worst. We see children when they are hungry, tired, energized, in a state of flow. We are the constant companions to the otherwise unseen moments that comprise the children's lives.

Imagine the following moments. A smile creeps across a child's face as they watch a caterpillar slink across a stalk of milkweed. Two best friends experiment with a new word or turn of phrase as they joke together out of our sight yet just within our earshot. A child's look of fear transforms into one of glee as they wade, barefoot, into a fresh, gooey puddle of mud. We all know moments like these, and as you think of these moments and of similar ones you have experienced in your context, you will likely see just how the dance between emic and etic—interpretations and ascriptions of meanings that come from within or outside of a culture, respectively—works in your engagements with young children. You'll have your ideas about their interactions, you'll make decisions to step in and support, you'll offer commentary based on your ideas about what is meaningful and, hopefully, you'll support them in identifying and gathering their own meaning from these interactions.

These moments are what I have taken to calling *otherwise unseen*—the moments that children may not remember or recall in detail, that parents do not know about given their absence during the school day, and that but for our witness to them would be forever lost.

THE POSITION OF A TEACHER

The position of an early childhood educator is unique among most or perhaps all others who work with young children. We are immersed in children's lives and cultures day in and day out. It is likely that we are engrossed in children's lives and cultures more than the lives and cultures of some of our adult counterparts. We are ethnographers, at the intersection of sociology, anthropology, and psychology, who are participant observers in a society whose rituals, norms, and ways of being, doing, speaking, creating, and relating both are and are not our own.

Seeing the Unseen Moments and Firsts

School settings and settings of care are unique contexts, and being present for children's lives as they unfold within these unique contexts is a gift that ought not be taken lightly. After all, we are the *only* ones who will ever see and potentially remember many of the firsts for the children in our care. We watch, with awe, as children attempt to make meaning with others, to create using materials, to grasp, utter, care, and more. Our proximity also gives us an intimate knowledge of children. Indeed, while it may sound controversial on the surface, I assert that within early settings of care and schooling, we know children better than their caregivers and families of origin.

Seeing Children as Members of Peer Groups

As teachers, we have the unique position of knowing children as they enter, integrate into, and navigate relationships, conflicts, triumphs, and growth within an extensive network of similarly aged peers. We are present for children's first steps into sustained peer relationships, with all of the humor, inquiry, conflict, and joy these entail.

It is Kyle's first day at NOLA Nature School. His first day, actually, at any school, ever. He is freshly turned three, and the first wave of the COVID-19 pandemic has given way to a second. However, in our corner of the forest, life proceeds as mostly normal. During lunchtime, Kyle, Rosemary, and I sit on a bench together. My phone is out, ready to document Kyle's first lunch at school. It is a norm among many educators to document these precious firsts in children's lives with the intention of sharing them with others. Kyle looks at Rosemary over lunch and puts his fingers into his cheek. Rosemary breaks out into laughter, and Kyle does the same. Twice more he repeats this, his smile widening as he removes his fingers from his mouth, his glances at Rosemary punctuated with giggles. It is his first connection of laughter with a friend in school.

This access is special, and this is only one example of the many firsts and foundational life events we see. We have access to children's successes and failures, to the bids that *almost* work and those that fall short of the mark. We hear the conversations between the two children who decide to be best friends and play only with each other long before those two children tell a third child, who we also know wants to be friends, that they can't play the camping game. We watch as children find their balance, stride, cruise, and ultimately walk and run, so to speak, in every aspect of development. We watch not only one child but very often *many* children on all sorts of days and in various spaces working together to create, solidify, sustain, and navigate all of the social nuance, intrigue, and (yes) scandal proper to any highly developed society.

Seeing Children as Intellectuals

As individuals who work with young children daily, we are also uniquely positioned to encounter and know children in communities of inquiry. For example, we are aware of which children love to share in a group and which prefer solo time to explore before sharing their ideas. We know (and, importantly, so do the children) who is good at drawing diagrams, who is good at leading a group, who is a faithful executor of tasks, and who doesn't mind getting dirty or taking a long walk to explore a new topic. And, what's more, we know how all the children interact when they are together.

Consider with me:

How do the communities of inquiry with which you come into contact construct knowledge?

Who prefers to share out loud? Who likes to process internally? Who do you call on to help rally the group? To figure out a way to solve a problem?

In some ways, this unique access to children's lives is understood. It is, after all, the reason why caregivers and families come to teachers for insights—and will often express surprise at the ways their children are different at school than at home. I want to invite us further along this path of thought, however, and assert that as early educators, our insight into children's lives is not only unique and well-informed by the nature of the time and social context within which we visit children, but it is also privileged.

Seeing Children in a Child-Centered Context

While out-of-school caregivers have the joy of bringing children out into the wide world, our role as teachers generally involves working with children in a context that is created with them in mind. *Privilege* isn't often a word we think of when we attempt to describe what it means to work with young children. Fulfilling? For sure. Loving? Often. Worthwhile? Always. Exhausting? Also always. Fun? Oh yeah. But privileged? Absolutely. We are privileged because the contexts within which we encounter children are contexts created *for* children both physically and otherwise. Rather than seeing children in the hustle and bustle of a busy market or in line for a ride at a theme park or in an airport in transit from one destination to another, we encounter children in a context made for them.

Think about it: the art materials in your classroom are within reach for children, the toilets and sinks are likely low enough for them to reach, and your schedule is, perhaps, padded with extra time for unanticipated transitions. Mentally, we have an expectation that things might take longer than expected, that there will be mess, and that we give ourselves and our children the time and space to clean it up. What this ultimately means is that the relationships, inquiry, and overall development that we observe are authentic, holistic, and valid—what our psychologist friends who follow in the tradition of Urie Bronfenbrenner might call "ecologically valid."

Contexts for children are, generally speaking, unhurried, giving children access to a variety of materials and offering them the freedom to explore and create with those materials in ways that blend and cross disciplines. As children create, develop, and grow, we educators also have privileged insight into the interconnectedness of children's ideas and experiences.

Also, depending on the image of the child that defines our practice, we also have the unique combination of an awareness of a child's unfolding development, a close relationship with that child and their peers, and the tools and insight to document and illuminate the ways that these relationships are influencing and influenced by context as well as progressing along each child's individual developmental trajectory. The access that we have to these child-centered spaces gives us a unique vision into the possibility of childhood.

Is it Possible to Access the "Authentic" Voices of Children?

Given the authenticity of these experiences, we can confidently say that as educators, we have access to the voices of children. We know what children sound like, we hear their concerns, we hear their dreams, we overhear their conversations with one another and their self-talk, and we are witnesses to things and ideas and creativity that are not present in any other context. We talk *with* children, and children trust us enough to share their ideas with us. This access to children's voices is one of the greatest privileges of our work. Of course, as Allison James (2001, 2007) reminds us, this access is not without its bias.

Indeed, however close we are to children, however immersed we are in their lives, contexts, and experiences, we can never fully inhabit a child's life or perspective in the same way that we can never fully inhabit the perspective of an individual we encounter on the street. I emphasize that having unique positioning does *not* mean that we understand everything about childhood fully. Instead, it refers to the fact that our proximity to children's lives and the cross-section we have of these lives means that our insights are unique and interesting and can meaningfully add to conversations about children and how they are in the world. Our positionalities as adults, with our jobs as educators, researchers, coordinators, and more, all mean that we still approach childhood through the lenses described in chapter 1 and therefore tend to hold images that coincide with our positioning. This is not meant to discourage us. On the contrary, I hope it leaves us curious and ever ready to examine our presuppositions and conclusions about what and who children are, why they do what they do, and what these each mean for our relationships with them.

The Necessity of Reflection

The benefits of reflective practice in early childhood have been lauded by authors, educators, philosophers, and researchers for decades. At their core, reflective practices involve thinking about what one does with and for children throughout the day and about the children themselves in more depth and detail than we typically have "in the moment." Reflection can occur during the moment that an interaction or situation is unfolding, afterward in community, or individually; they are often also a precursor to the formal reports and summaries that we provide in conferences, other official communications with families, and so on.

Reflection (and the processing that often accompanies it) is absolutely indispensable if we hope to be able to use the unique positioning that we have in children's lives to invite these critical conversations.

What might you do to facilitate reflection within your center? If you are a director, where can you build in or expand upon opportunities for reflection among your staff?

POSSIBILITIES

So where might this leave us? We are uniquely positioned, and yet we cannot know everything. So what do we even do with the things that we can know, do know, or are finding out? I see at least two possibilities.

The first possibility is that we can keep all of these things to ourselves and put them in a box; we leave it alone and don't let it inform our practice. Yes, we know children are interesting, and yes, we understand that we are uniquely close to them, but we don't do anything about it.

I don't like that one.

The other possibility is that we strive to figure out a way through, a way to look at and frame the experiences of childhood: for children (because it is their lives we are considering), for ourselves (as those who spend significant time with them), and for others (who are forming and re-forming ideas about childhood, what it means, and what it ought to look like).

This second position also implies that we are using this proximity to its full advantage, drawing threads between the continuities from moment to moment and day to day that our closeness to children affords us the opportunity to see.

This is the one that I think is best.

And, interestingly enough, many if not most of us are already doing it to some degree. Let's consider how.

PUTTING OUR UNIQUE POSITIONING TO USE

As mentioned previously, there is already, at least among educators, an implicit recognition of teachers' privileged access to children's lives, a privilege and uniqueness afforded not only by expertise and training but also by proximity to children. With this unique privilege of proximity to the otherwise unseen, teachers tend to do at least three things: they share, they reflect, and they love. We love the children with whom we work in part because we know them so well. This sharing, reflecting, and expressing of love occur internally and externally in both informal and formal ways.

INTERNAL INFORMAL	EXTERNAL INFORMAL
The wonderings you have about your children that you share with other educators in your community.	Conferences and meetings between educators and caregivers outside of formally delineated times. Reflecting, sharing experiences in conversations over coffee, at happy hour, and so on.
INTERNAL FORMAL	EXTERNAL FORMAL
Communications between educators and administrators about children. May not immediately be shared with parents/families.	Planned conferences and meetings between educators and caregivers or educators and external colleagues, such as regional or national conferences, working groups and communities of practice, and so on.

Internal Informal: Impromptu Wonderings

One of the ways that, among ourselves, educators acknowledge this privileged position is in our sharing with one another. How often do you observe something funny, interesting, or concerning happening in your classroom with the children? Who is the first person with whom you share your reflection? The likely answer is with a colleague, perhaps a coteacher or a friend on staff. This sort of internal, informal sharing of anecdotes, observations, and wonderings—nearly constantly— is not only critical for understanding the children with whom we work but also a natural result of the privileged access we have to children's lives. We wonder so deeply because, explicitly or implicitly, we are aware of and intrigued by the complexity of the lives and experiences we observe.

I am spending the morning in the Green Dragonfly classroom at Newtowne School in Cambridge, Massachusetts. I am kneeling on the floor as I sit next to Joao, who is writing letters to various members of his family and, most recently, a friend's younger sibling. Even among four-year-olds, it seems, it is valuable to connect to others in friends' lives. While I sit with Joao, I notice my fellow teacher Lori walks past me into the little alcove just out of my sight. When she emerges, I say, "Wow, it seems like the Cozy Room is really popping off today."

"Yeah!" she says, gesturing over for me to look at the phone.

I rise and she turns the screen to show me the picture. Numbers, shapes, and sloping and swooping lines overlap atop a lit light table. Dry-erase markers are strewn about the tabletop, signs of the children's work. Lori's intrigue is apparent, and I can tell a thousand wonders are firing off in her head at any given moment.

Internal Formal: Communicating with Others

As educators, we are often required to communicate formally with others inside of our institutions. This may involve taking some of our impromptu noticings or wonderings and drawing parallels between them so we can meet a particular standard our center sets.

One example of an internal occasion for formal sharing is an internal review. Here we might observe our own practices or those of others and then collect our thoughts in a formal way. Perhaps we are focusing on the experience of a particular child or subgroup of children or evaluating the way a new space is being used or how a new set of pedagogical philosophies is being implemented.

External Informal: Work and Life Intersect

Simply speaking, externally and informally, our unique position allows us to say certain things about children and childhood with authority or experience that we might otherwise not be able to. For example, at a happy hour with a brave friend who has brought her toddler along, I am able to talk about everyday life and, moments later, share with her some things I've been thinking about related to the wide range of aesthetic sensibilities I've been noticing in toddlers in my classroom and that I notice in her toddler.

External Formal: Outward-Facing Communications

This privileged access is most explicitly acknowledged during communication with parents, often at regular intervals, the forms of meetings, check-ins, or conferences where teachers share their insights into children's development as they have witnessed it. Even the term *conference* suggests the formal sharing of findings that one has gathered about a particular subject, topic, or idea. In the case of our work, these subjects are children, the topics are the topics that make up their lives and experiences, and the ideas are our thoughts on everything from the typicality, creativity, and overall levels of interest that make up their days with us.

An excerpt from a conference form:

It has been a pleasure to watch as Ian forges a close friendship with Kyle and Griff, cemented by their mutual interest in war games, building, wrestling, and climbing. In fact, Ian's climbing has even inspired Griff and Kyle to work on their skills as well! This is just one illustration of the sort of gentle leadership that Ian exemplifies.

In each of these contexts, we are using our unique position as adults in tune with and attuned to children's experiences to provide valuable insights into their lives to those who care most about them: their caregivers, ourselves included! No one else has this cross-section of experience—a view of both forest and trees, bird's-eye and ant-level.

UNIQUE POSITIONALITY AS A TOOL FOR TRANSLATION

We can begin to see, then, that our position provides us with access not only to children's lives and experiences but also to a unique intersection of knowledges that few, if any, others enjoy. We are constantly gathering, reflecting on, and interpreting a multitude of information on childhoods from a broad range of sources across time. Pedagogically, we know what developmental and educational research and theories suggest, as well as which ways we choose to accommodate and resist those suggestions. We also know about caregivers and parents and have access to their insights on parenting and caregiving styles, the priorities and obligations of caregiving, and how the priorities and practices of individual caregivers are related to their underlying hopes, dreams, and aspirations for their children. We also see how priorities and anxieties shift and morph in response to events on local and national scales and other factors.

In addition to this, we are also present for children's lives and, as mentioned above, are continually receiving and integrating vast amounts of information about them. Further, as we consider the information we gather about children and their families, we would be remiss if we removed ourselves from the equation. After all, we are participant observers in these systems, and we form a central piece of the educational architecture that is under our study.

I want, then, to propose that we conceptualize ourselves as translators or interpreters. We are translating between the children in our classrooms and the broader school community; we are translating between children and their caregivers (and vice versa); and we are also translating between the structures and arrangements of our classrooms and broader societal ideas about children, school, and children's lives. We are at the nexus of all these intersecting domains, and by the very nature of our work, we are required to take a serious look at each one.

We are participant researchers whose findings and insights are relevant not only in the lives of our classrooms and as they relate to children but also to the broader discourse on children and childhoods. Of course we all have our own biases, our own lenses and frameworks that give color to our thinking. And yes, we each have some domains that motivate us toward engagement more than others. The point is that whatever those domains and our motivations for sharing are, we are uniquely positioned to ask and answer critical questions regarding children, the way they experience and construct cultures of childhood, and the intersections of these cultures with broader features of our world and society.

CRITICAL QUESTIONS

When we think beyond conferences, beyond the formal and informal ways we share, we might wonder at the possibilities. What potentials are at our fingertips? It would be remiss of us to use a deeper, more nuanced understanding of childhood to speak only to the same things. Of course information on fine- and gross-motor skills is valuable, knowing colors helps children communicate in ways that are easier for adults to understand, and socioemotional development is a critical piece of a child's life and experience. Yet as educator ethnographers whose access to children, their lives, and experiences also intersects with an understanding of days and moments that are inexhaustibly rich, we can do more.

Our unique positioning as witnesses to the deep richness that is otherwise unseen means that we can begin to approach deep questions. What's more, we can approach these questions with deeper context.

For example, we can ask questions like these:

How are children living out childhood in my community?

How are the children in conversation with societal ideas and conversations, and what implications does this have?

What can we learn from the children about what it means to be a child in contemporary society? In our particular space and time?

We could even wonder: What knowledges are children revealing through their creative endeavors? How can art itself represent the knowledges that children hold about the world? What gaze do children take toward artistic materials? To illustrate exactly what I mean, I invite you to come with me back to the classroom.

It was one of those days when only three children of our typical ten showed up to school. A couple were sick, some were traveling, others were out of town or having a "special stay home day" as we called it. At its core, however, what that meant was that we had three children that day, and it was glorious. The three children present that day were all avid artists.

It is also important to note that these four-year-olds had spent nearly half of their lives in a world ravaged by COVID-19, meaning that they had observed the adults in their lives navigate their way through video calls and virtual workdays.

Therefore, given this intersection between artistic prowess and familiarity with the world of virtual communication, Rosemary's decision to draw a computer might not come as a surprise. At first coteacher Lauren and I weren't sure what the lines, drawn with utmost intention, meant—however, it was soon clear. One half of her folded sheet of watercolor paper (thick enough to support itself when folded, unlike regular printer paper) was covered in squarish-rectangular boxes.

On the other side of her paper, however, Rosemary surprised us by drawing a detailed picture of her dad.

"Hello, my name is Chris!" she mimicked, sending me, Lauren, and her peers into peals of laughter. Little did we know that this innovation would prove to be the beginning of what feels most appropriately referred to as an artistic movement or period, perhaps "the Computer Period."

In the coming days and weeks, children made their own computers—Cara made one featuring her mom, Laura added games to her computer, and Louis built on both of these developments, incorporating dinosaur video games into his computer.

In their work, the children demonstrated a degree of expertise manipulating small objects—a valuable indicator of fine-motor skills. In many cases, the children also revealed at least implicit knowledge of shapes and colors as they decided just how wide and tall to make the squares they drew and exactly which color dots ought to go on the page.

Looking through a different lens, the children also revealed a love of art, a desire for and enjoyment of creative work. They also revealed an appreciation for conducting this sort of work side by side—in parallel.

However, another lens has a different light to shed on this interaction.

These computers were part of a conversation. Through art the children were offering a commentary on their worlds. For Rosemary, her commentary had a

Right: Rosemary's piece, in progress. Felt-tipped pen on card stock.

Above: Rosemary working on her piece.

Facing page:
Louis working on the computer game.

Louis's computer game, featuring dinosaurs.
Felt-tipped pen on card stock.

satirical hue, lampooning her father's interactions in the virtual world. For Cara, her art was a commentary on her mother's beauty—her words, explicitly, were "Look how beautiful my mom is." Laura and Louis were in conversation with the digital aspects of their lives. In particular, from my conversations with his family, I knew that Louis was only allowed to play video games and watch television as part of a community—these were special times with his dad.

I like to wonder if, in his interpretation of Rosemary's original artifact (depicting a parent), Louis decided to depict an activity he engaged in *with* his parent—his dad, though off-screen in the physical rendering, is psychologically present *with* him. Is this the case? Or is it nothing of the sort?

The goal is not to answer the question definitively, but to use our proximity—to see the trend, to know the cultural context, to speak with and listen to children, to understand how their activities and explorations gain traction within their social and relational networks—to ask big questions.

As teachers, we had the gift of becoming ever more aware of the complexities of our classrooms' cultural milieu. We had watched the start of this practice, rooted in a typical norm, and we saw how it became both a medium of conversation and a sustained piece of creativity and play that evolved in exciting and intriguing directions over the course of weeks.

Our access as educators, it is worth repeating, is so unique and so privileged that we are well-positioned to answer questions that go far deeper than the baseline. We could have stopped at shape identification. We might have been tempted to highlight the fine-motor development. But we would have missed the stories.

We would also not have been able to capture these stories had we not documented them with intention. Yes, I could have snapped a picture or written a sentence, and that would have said *something* about what happened here. But what would it have missed? How can we document in ways that do justice to the proximity we have to children? How might we document children's lives and experiences in ways that construct and contribute to strong images of children living immensely rich lives?

Reflections

In what ways have you in the past thought about what it means to be a teacher or educator?

How have your understandings of what it is possible to see, do, and understand as an educator changed?

In what ways might an educator who is attuned to their role as translator/interpreter be positioned to support families? What might be important for an educator/interpreter to learn from families in order to more meaningfully interpret the experiences that unfold within the context of the school day?

Chapter 4

Lens and Frame: Documentation as Ethnography

INTRODUCTION: IMMERSED IN CHILDREN'S WORLDS

In the following chapter, we explore the resonances between documentation and ethnographic fieldwork. While we acknowledge that the relationship between documentation and ethnography is not one-to-one, we also examine how the practices of documentation and ethnography are more aligned than many might initially expect. We begin by defining documentation and ethnography and then proceed to compare and contrast documentation and ethnography as typically defined. Next, we wonder: How are early childhood educators like ethnographers? What features of their experiences in classrooms each day mirror those of ethnographers who are immersed in, interacting with, and influenced by a culture other than their own? In the second part of the chapter, we consider some practical pieces of what might inform ethnographically framed documentation. We close with a consideration of how to position ourselves as adults and educators within an ethnographic narrative. How might our decisions to foreground ourselves or not within our documentation influence the ways that a narrative is encountered in the world?

~

FRAMING OUR WORK

A frame is both a useful and a not-so-useful metaphor. Frames give context, adorning and highlighting aspects of a piece of art or an artifact—and they also reveal a concrete limitation and boundary. They constrain and accentuate, hide and reveal. A lens, in a similar way, filters our view of a work, artifact, or event. It can be specific or nonspecific; it can filter in, filter out, or filter in a way that shifts color and hue. It is also a useful yet incomplete metaphor.

My intention is not to resolve this tension but merely to introduce and acknowledge it. By framing our documentation of children's lives as ethnographic work, we give prominence to certain aspects of this practice as we exclude others. By viewing our documentation practice through an ethnographic lens, we are invited into a point of view that means we will end up emphasizing certain aspects of practice and experience and deemphasizing or according less space to others—said otherwise, we all have things we'll focus on and things we won't. There is no perfect balance, but I do believe and hope to convince you that viewing documentation within an ethnographic frame and through an ethnographic lens is more beneficial than detrimental.

We begin in the forest. A low swing hangs from the branch of a large old oak tree. A group of children gathers on one side of the swing, their bodies forming two wavy lines along either side of what ultimately will be the trajectory of the swing.

All eyes are on Jon, a curly-haired five-year-old, who stands directly across from the other children on the other side of the swing. Jon's mouth tilts up in a smile and his eyes glint with what I can only imagine is a hint of preemptive pride in the feat he is about to achieve.

"Three!" Jon shouts. A giggle erupts from his gathered classmates.

"Two!" he says, leaning over in what looks like a runner's stance—arms bent at sharp angles at the elbow. The other children are jumping.

"One!" In this moment, word and movement are the same, and Jon races forward, lunges toward the swing, and lands on the seat of the swing with his belly. As he moves forward and back, the other children begin to run in front of the swing, barely missing Jon's body. This is, of course, is the whole point—not to get hit, not to *not* be hit, but to just miss being hit.

Documentation and ethnography are both investigative practices that involve gathering information in multiple modalities or forms that sheds light on a particular practice, process, or people that is shared broadly (both with the population contributing to the study and beyond) for the sake of building knowledge, changing perspective, and informing future actions and interactions. Each is an act of communication, a lantern, a snapshot into an experience. In the next sections, I'll define *documentation* and *ethnography*, consider the similarities and differences between them, and reflect on some ways this frame is beneficial as we strive to capture children's lives. I'll also talk about some first and fledgling steps toward practically applying this ethnographic frame.

DEFINITIONS OF DOCUMENTATION

Mara Krechevsky and her colleagues offer a thorough definition of documentation. They write that documentation "involves teachers and learners in observing, recording, interpreting, and sharing via a variety of media the processes and products of learning in order to deepen and extend learning" (Krechevsky et al. 2013, 59). Documentation might also be described as the fruit (or result) of a deep respect for children that "value[s] children's ideas, thinking, questions, and theories about the world," which it discerns through collecting "traces of [children's] work" that are interpreted, shared broadly, and used to deepen learning both within and beyond the classroom (2013, 1). Documentation is a close look at children's lives, or some aspect of them, that is shared. Documentation is not something that we keep to ourselves.

The privileged access we have to the voices, lives, and experiences of children, as well as our obligations to act as translator for their actions for others and to provide opportunities for others to encounter those voices, means that documentation is nearly inevitable even if not explicitly required in some form or another. I like to consider documentation as a dynamic artifact made up of dynamic artifacts. It considers moments and experiences that we have engaged in with children, witnessed alongside children, or observed occurring within individuals or groups of children. Documentation then seeks to translate these moments and experiences through artifacts in multiple modalities, making them visible and intelligible in a context outside of which they originally occurred (Edwards, Gandini, and Forman 2012). And it does this through a variety of ways. Documentation (1) asks questions, (2) gathers information across multiple media and modes, (3) sheds light on people/processes/practices, (4) is interpreted (ideally in collaboration), and (5) is then shared in a way that allows further and future thought.

✦ Documentation asks questions.

What do the children know about games with rules? How are they using these rules to reinforce the existing power dynamics within the classroom? Are there ways we might challenge the children to be more inclusive and/or flexible in their play?

✦ Documentation gathers information across multiple modalities.

A page in my journal with the heading "12/15 | Cloudy | #mulchmtns #games" details a conversation between the children as they are playing the perennial game of good guys versus bad guys. In addition, photos and video from that day also

"I played that game."

"It's a game with sticks and fighting."

12-15-20

Title: "I played that game. It's a game with sticks and fighting."

Artist: Rosemary (age 4).

Medium: Red marker on white printer paper.

What might she have meant by playing? What might this drawing, and her words about it, reveal about the way she perceived and/ or felt during this game?

show the children sitting down discussing in a fort. A child's drawing that day (a child, notably, who wasn't playing the game) shows a picture with the transcription, "I played that game. It's a game with sticks and fighting" (Rosemary, 12/15/2020).

✦ Documentation sheds light on people, processes, and practices.

William loved to play with his friends and also, in the same vein, loved to be the decision maker in these games. One day I documented how he took the role of decision maker and used his power to change the location of the "Safety Stone" (the term he coined for what children often call the "base"). He changed the Safety Stone once, twice, three times, four times. With each shift, his classmates became increasingly frustrated. Eventually, William relented and kept the Safety Stone in one place.

✦ Documentation is interpreted in collaboration.

Documentation is interpreted, ideally, between teachers and children, each of whose voice brings different hues and perspectives to the investigation under consideration. Not only do teachers contribute various sorts of data—for example, the drawing described above was noticed (and the words transcribed) by my coteacher while I was observing the other group of children—but they also contribute perspectives that challenge, confirm, or refine thinking on a topic.

✦ Documentation is shared.

Finally, documentation is shared—with children, with colleagues, with community (including families and other invested and interested members of the community). This sharing can, and often does, lead to further questions and inquiry, inspiring communities of educators to, again, ask questions, gather more information, and see where the light can be shed again and again and again.

DOCUMENTATION AS ETHNOGRAPHY: NEW VIEWS OF CHILDHOOD

What if we shared our documentation in ways that not only made learning visible but also invited others to consider children and childhood in new ways? What if the ways in which we saw children, framed the values of their lives and experiences, and listened to their voices extended outside of the bounds of our typical frameworks and perspectives?

As we begin to chart our ways toward some of the many possible answers to these questions, it might be helpful, again, to draw some inspiration from our colleagues in sociology and anthropology, whose ethnography shares many parallels with our documentation. This connection likely comes as no surprise. Chapter 1 touches on how the perspectives on sociology, anthropology, and education come together to construct our images of the child; in chapter 2, I borrow the terms *emic* and *etic* as I argue for an ongoing practice of approaching children's lives in a way that emphasizes the children's own intentions and interpretations rather than our own; and in chapter 3, I position educators as proximate researchers who have the opportunity to observe, in depth, a variety of cultural phenomena that are simultaneously familiar and foreign. In the same way, I want to challenge us to ponder the potential of an ethnographically inspired practice of documentation.

But first: What do we mean when we say *ethnography*?

Defining Ethnography

Ethnography is typically a term reserved for research in sociology and anthropology that takes what might be termed an up-close view of a subject—a group of people and/or a practice of their society/culture. In the *Handbook of Ethnography*, Allison James (2001, 1) writes that ethnography, put simply, "means writing about people." Jenny Ritchie (2019, 2), writing for the *Oxford Research Encyclopedia of Education*, adds that ethnographies "provide rich, in-depth understandings of the cultural beliefs and practices of particular groups of people." This understanding, in ethnographic practice, is gained through sustained, up-close, and personal interaction with members of a community and participation in their lives (James 2007; Ritchie 2019), and it is this proximity that lends credibility to the ethnography being constructed (James 2007). Through "systematic naturalistic observation of children . . . in their routine settings" (LeVine 2007, 250–51), ethnography affords an "opportunity to discover, in an emergent, responsive way . . . intricate dynamics of interactions"—a discovery that anthropologist Robert LeVine goes on to suggest is based in ongoing interaction and sustained presence.

James (2001) offers a thorough account of the development of ethnography as a method for studying children and childhood, tracing its comingled scientific and colonial roots (see box on p. 68) from the anthropological studies in the late nineteenth and early twentieth centuries to more contemporary work where an increased focus on children's lives and experiences has, she argues, opened the door for the concept of children as active participants in their socialization and that despite an early emphasis on positioning children as human beings who were merely en route to adulthood, modern ethnographies have increasingly acknowledged and sought to provide color to the active participation and agency that children exercise in their experiences of socialization.

The Racist and Colonial Roots of Anthropology and Ethnography

I would be remiss not to acknowledge and to officially decry the reductionist, colonial, and racist histories of many historical pioneers and exponents of ethnography. This practice is not historically neutral. It was often used by individuals situated within European empires to explore the practices of individuals whose countries were colonized. Ethnographers often referred to subjects and participants as "savages," comparing the practices of various Indigenous groups (across the entire globe) to what they considered to be a superior (that is, White and Eurocentric) culture. These reductive perspectives are, in many ways, an inextricable piece of the history of ethnography and are something with which we must wrestle as we consider the utility of this lens and frame today.

With all of this this in mind, what I hope to offer here is my own addition to the chorus of voices who have been exploring and expanding notions of participant ethnography, where the individuals whose community is under study are recognized as full-fledged human beings and participants in the research process, and whose practices are not regarded as less-than, uncivilized, or otherwise inferior to some arbitrary standard. Instead, I advocate for an ethnography rooted in respect and admiration—centered on the desire to illuminate the beauty present within the processes we see unfolding. If anyone is interested in notions of this sort of research, Eve Tuck's 2009 piece on damage-centered research is a valuable place to begin, as is any work of portraiture by Sara Lawrence-Lightfoot (Lawrence-Lightfoot and Hoffmann Davis 1997).

The Early Childhood Educator as Ethnographer

If, as James (2001) suggests, an important component of the credibility of ethnographies is derived from immersion of ethnographers in the daily lives of the subjects—that is, of the children—under study, then by virtue of their immersion in children's daily lives and doings, educators are well-positioned to employ ethnographic methods and perspectives. As mentioned in the previous chapter, educators are uniquely positioned to obtain information about the population under consideration, to learn about the contexts surrounding the daily lives of that population, to develop relationships with and to be trusted by the population under consideration, and to document and share with others the insights gleaned from and co-created with that population.

Ritchie (2019, 8) suggests that early childhood education is a field that can particularly benefit from ethnography, writing that the "sensitive understanding[s]" that ethnography affords early childhood educators (that is, in terms of cultural ideas, practices, and norms) can contribute to deeper relationships with families and, thereby, contribute to children's well-being as well. We might also add that this sensitivity to children's experiences can contribute in a direct way to the enrichment of our relationships with children.

In addition, Ritchie (2019) suggests that ethnographies have the potential to give voice to young children—voice that has, within many disciplines, often been erased or sidelined, even and especially by well-intentioned adults (Yoon and Templeton 2019). Here we might pause to ponder how this might relate to our understandings of children and childhood and either accord with or challenge the images we have of children as competent and fully realized humans capable of a variety of modes of self-expression and nuanced understandings of complex social interactions.

Mary Jane Moran makes the explicit connection that educators "must develop new skills, including those typically associated with the role of ethnographer" (1997, 212)—but she leaves it there. Deb Curtis and Margie Carter (2022) remind us to look closely at things as they are happening *now*, with the children's perspectives in mind. Similarly we are reminded not to impose our own meanings on data gathered from the field but instead to wonder what the things we see mean to the group (the children) we are observing.

TRADITIONAL DOCUMENTATION AND ETHNOGRAPHY COMPARED

There is, however, at least one important difference between more traditional ethnographic work with young children and the work of ethnographically inspired documentation as championed here. One of the great benefits of ethnographic work with children is that the researcher is able to remain in proximity to the child (that is, has access to the child) without having the responsibilities of the educator. Traditional researchers are not teachers or educators and do not need to pause note-taking or observation to help with drop-off or pickup or to turn their attention away from the group they are observing if, for example, a conflict erupts across the room. Within schools, early childhood ethnographers can maintain a distance from daily life and from responsibility that is simply impossible for educators. However, this inability to remain at a distance—the reality that, as educators, we are also playmate, authority figure, thought leader, and more, all at the same time—does not need to hinder our work and can even be a strength.

Think about it:

How might the care we have for and the responsibilities we have toward children actually aid us in gathering together insights from and into their lives and experiences?

Another difference between the work of educators and ethnographers involves power, setting, and access. James notes that issues of power, setting, access, and context must be considered when researchers carry out ethnographic fieldwork with young children. In particular, she explores the power dynamics of adults and children, the constraints of fieldwork conducted in school settings or at home, and the issues of access that come along with work carried out in either context (James 2007). For example, Ritchie (2019) notes that when consent is gained to participate in ethnographic research, it is often the adult gatekeepers who have made the decisions that children can and will participate. Both Ritchie and James make note of how important it is, nonetheless, to consult children about their participation, striving as much as possible to obtain their consent or dissent.

As educators, our relationships with children are likely already very close, meaning that we have both access to children and often have or can easily obtain their consent for sending photos to families and caregivers, sharing stories with them, and so on. We also have permission for this proximity given to us directly by the families themselves—often at the start of the year in an official form and implicitly each day as families entrust the care and well-being of their children to us. However, we might learn from researchers what it looks like and how it feels to gain true consent from a child to tell their story. Perhaps it is a practice we integrate before sharing a snapshot, or we consult a child about whether they would prefer us to convey a story in their presence or in private.

As teachers who are also researchers, we are not exempt from the dance between our desire to do what is best for children and accountability to external standards with which we may not agree. Sociologists Peter F. Harvey and Annette Lareau (2020, 17) refer to this as "the double act" and "walking the tightrope." However, our dance looks different. We are accountable to families and to children and to our program, and we exist within the space of an invested nonfamilial adult who is, nonetheless, one of the people who sees and knows a child best. It is messy—and wonderful.

And, finally, in an important note, Ritchie (2019, 10) encourages researchers to maintain relationships, "to give back as much as they receive from the early childhood center community in which they are engaged for their project." As teachers who are integrating ethnographic perspective into our documentation practice, we would do well to take a similar path, consulting children on which pieces of their experiences can and should be included in documentation and how. This giving back also includes the gift of our continued and ongoing attention. Said otherwise, it means that our interaction is not over when we have documented what we came to document—especially not if a child asks us to document something further. Perhaps you intended to and successfully did document an art exploration—but after you put away your camera and notes, a child invites you over to the slide and asks you to take a picture of them on the slide. Do it! In this way, we ensure that our documentation practice is not extractive—we are, again, not done merely when *we* decide to be done, but when we are sure the children truly feel respected, honored, and satisfied with these interactions.

Mutually Beneficial Documentation

What are some ways you might ensure that your documentation practice is not extractive? How can you make the experience of documenting children's lives beneficial to the children being documented? Some of the practices listed below may support you along the way to doing this. You might, for example, consider:

- Inviting children to contribute to as many pieces of documentation as they can. Children will not only see that they are being talked about but also be able to have conversations with others about themselves.
- Inviting children to decide which photographs are included in a display.
- Discussing with children the meaning of documentation that you create/co-create.

These differences notwithstanding, there are still a plethora of similarities between documentation and ethnography. Documentation and ethnography are both investigative practices that consider multiple modes of data in constructing a final text, image, or series of texts and images, and pedagogical documentation and ethnographic fieldwork both draw on their proximity to the subjects participating in research for their credibility. Further, documentation and ethnographic fieldwork share the following characteristics.

✦ **Documentation and ethnography each shed light on particular practices, processes, or groups.**

Both pedagogical documentation and ethnographic fieldwork take everyday happenings and encourage us to reframe and re-understand what it is we are seeing. Either may involve deconstructing a practice, habit, or way of being, rendering it both familiar and strange so that those who encounter the experience, while forever secondhand, can extract the essence of what has been observed. This close gaze implicitly declares, "I value you; I value your action in the world."

✦ **Each is, ideally, shared broadly—both with the population contributing to the study and beyond.**

Ethnographies, and the research that precedes and coexists alongside them, are produced for the sake of building knowledge, changing perspectives, and informing future actions and interactions. Ritchie (2019), for example, cites researchers whose ethnographies of childhood in child care contexts contributed to discourse that, in subsequent years, became the movement away from strictly standards-based institutions. Similarly, the insights gained from pedagogical documentation inform teaching practices, help educators turn a critical eye to institutional norms, and help adults (and children) evaluate and reevaluate the activities and practices in which they participate daily.

✦ **Early childhood educators and ethnographers conducting field research share common methods.**

We have already mentioned how deeply enmeshed in their subjects' and participants' lives ethnographers are and have drawn an explicit parallel between the proximity of ethnographers and that of early childhood educators to the lives of their research subjects or participants. This shared proximity, naturally, lends itself to similar methods. Educators interweave field notes, more extensive observational anecdotes, photographs, and artifacts, all in the service of constructing a picture of a culture and group with whom they share proximity. Educators, like ethnographers, form deep, complex relationships with the individuals they are studying and use these relationships to inform the narratives they weave.

AN "EVERYDAY ETHNOGRAPHY"

At this point in our journey together through this book, it feels valuable to focus on concrete adult practices—what does documentation as ethnography actually look like day to day?

The reality is that it is often less in the products themselves and more in the questions we ask about the products we see and co-create with children. In diving into this point, I'd like us to consider two forms of representation: two-dimensional photography and videography and three-dimensional representations (including children's drawings). I chose to focus our attention on these as they are among the most commonly used to document children's lives and development.

Other features of qualitative ethnographic fieldwork are useful to incorporate into our framing of documentation practice as we strive to say new and different things about children and childhood.

In Two Dimensions

Cushions in the Cozy Room: A Photo Essay

Friday, December 9, 2022, Newtowne School

At 9:28 a.m., three four-year-olds, Kevin, Rhea, and Yohan, are in the Cozy Room (just off the main classroom, filled with books about emotions, soft surfaces, and a light table). The trio appears to be conversing intently, with increasingly brusque tones (that I am not close enough to decode) reaching my ears with each passing second. I watch them from a few feet away, splitting my attention between them and Sal, who has enlisted my help to write a letter to a friend's baby sibling. After a minute or two, teacher Lori arrives in the Cozy Room, phone in hand, poised to take a picture of what I later learn is a collaborative piece of art the children created on the light table. By 9:33, Kevin and Rhea have grabbed two of the cushions behind Yohan. I start recording. I am able to capture the moment where Kevin and Rhea slam the cushions together and the broad smiles they wear as they do so. I capture Yohan extending his left hand up in what almost appears to be an attempt to stop Kevin from bumping into him, rolling onto his back and lifting up his legs so that the cushions Rhea and Kevin are sparring with collide with one another, and with Yohan's feet. Moments later, Lori asks the children to leave the room—the game is better played outside. Immediately I wonder, "Priorities! What would the children have to say about this?" I am left in my wonder, however, as the signal comes that it is time to clean up in preparation for morning gathering.

With smartphones readily at hand, photographs and videos are everywhere these days. While democratizing the practice, this proliferation also makes it tempting to dismiss the potential power that a photograph or video can hold—after all, if there are hundreds, what makes any one photo or video so special? Yet when captured with intention, at close proximity, a photograph has the potential to distill an experience into a single moment or into a series of its most significant moments.

In *Doing Visual Ethnography*, researcher Sara Pink (2021, 40) describes visual ethnography as "a dynamic, reflexive, and situated field of practice which involves researchers engaging with visual and digital methods and media in seeking to collaboratively create and share new ways of knowing and knowledge relating to specific research questions and agenda." In short, visual ethnography opens up new ways to co-create knowledge and embraces the digital and visual culture in which we now live. In the framework that Pink articulates, she suggests that visual ethnography, while not a replacement for text-based ethnography, offers a valuable expansion of the practice and concept of ethnographic work. Visual ethnography, according to Pink, is open to interpretation as well. This interpretation depends heavily on the context within which a visual artifact is presented and encountered. Pink writes, "Photographic meanings are contingent and subjective; they depend on who is looking, the temporalities and social and cultural contexts through which they are looking, and the dominant discourses, relations of power and ethics that surround them" (90).

Take a look, for example, at these photographs of a child using tape. What do they mean? What is their significance? The answer, of course, is "It depends."

The meaning of the photographs depends on what your experiences are with children with tape and what you believe about a child's need (or lack thereof) to use copious amounts of tape.

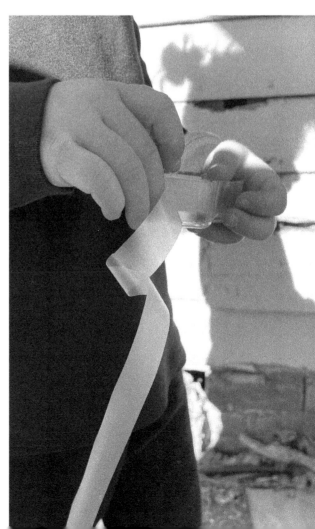

The fate of
the tape.

Visual methods, including photography and videography, can occupy multiple meanings. This reality invites us to engage with an expansive concept of literacy—often referred to as "literacies"—and asks us to challenge our initial assertions about how literacy can look as well. That is, given that young children are often invited to create, think in, and encounter texts through visual imagery (especially the pictures, photographs, and other sorts of drawings often featured in picture books), the image constitutes a legitimate textual form. One wonders if documentation that emphasizes tenets and aspects of visual ethnography—that embraces the image—could become the more desirable methodological form in our work with young children in classrooms and other contexts.

Typically, I use both photography and videography to capture moments, especially because with smartphones it is easy to switch between the two. However, when it comes time to synthesize these pieces into a coherent narrative, it is useful to consider the following:

What am I hoping to illuminate here? For whom and where will this be encountered?

How will video enhance the experience of the audience in encountering the moment being depicted?

If I use photography, which pieces of experience will I focus in on? What story will the series of photographs or the focus of the photographs tell?

Is it valuable to switch between these forms? What can be gained—or what is lost—in either format?

Rich documentation can, and ideally should, include "images, voices, sounds, and other perceptible traces from an experience" that will "evoke emotions as well as intellectual thought" (Krechevsky et al. 2013, 80). Next, we consider what these "traces" might look like.

In Three Dimensions

Three-dimensional artifacts offer unique insights into practices and people. We can learn about their sensibilities, including their priorities for form, function, aesthetic, utility, durability, and similar qualities. We might be able to see other markers of a physical presence, such as fingerprints that give us a clue as to the maker's size, orientation, flexibility, the depth of force with which they created a given artifact, and so on. And, given our unique proximity to children, we often have the luxury of watching the process of creation unfold before our very eyes!

We can watch the track of the child's eyes as they choose and manipulate a material. We can look on, participate even, as a certain way of folding paper, holding scissors, or using dot markers potentiates through a network of children, giving rise to a new series of practices and revealing a new way to visualize ink on paper.

Title: *The instrument.*

Artist: Ernest, age four.

Medium: Cardboard, paper, straw, masking tape.

The Instrument

November 22, 2022, Newtowne School

Around 9 a.m. in late November, on my first day among the three- and four-year-old class at Newtowne School in Cambridge, Mass., I decide it is time to move to a new area of the room. I have spent the first half hour of my time here speaking and playing with children on the meeting rug, and as my goal today is to get around to as many children and as many sections of the room as I can, I need to get moving. I decide on the area of the room where the activity seems highest and, I'll admit, my interest is greatest: the Workshop.

When I arrive at the Workshop—a table outfitted with loose parts, tape, slices of cardboard, and clipboards with graph

paper—Ernest is already hard at work, creating something the names of which I do not know. I watch as he affixes a blue straw that is impaling a brown section of paper-towel holder onto a piece of paper using three long pieces of bright-orange masking tape. He brings the contraption to his mouth.

Aiko, who has been working next to him for some time, creates a similar contraption. A photograph reveals that as Ernest lifts his creation to his face, Aiko is already holding the yellow masking tape in her hand—when, I wonder, was she inspired to create her own? A photo with a time stamp three minutes later reveals Aiko's creation—similar in form but entirely different in intention.

Ernest, I later learned, created an instrument, inspired by a visit from his music teacher the day before. Aiko, using a similar form, created a candle.

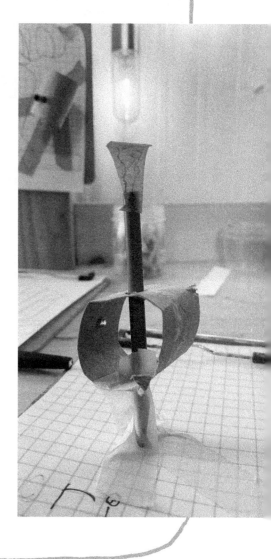

Title: *The candle*

Artist: Aiko, age four years, four months.

Medium: Cardboard, paper, straw, masking tape.

For each child, the experience of the singular event—the visit of the music teacher—activated a different response. Or perhaps they began with the same initial response and then built on and extended it in different ways. To be a child in this space, in the Workshop today, means that we are using straws and tape and paper to create three-dimensional representations. It means that we are experimenting with this form—straw, roll, tape, paper.

In these moments, it is valuable to consider what the ways of creating tell us about the disposition of the child and how we can contextualize that disposition with what we know about the broader culture of childhood as it exists within our classrooms. This is beyond any curricular goal, apart from any individualized assessment or evaluation of a child's so-called ability—we adopt a gaze similar to the one we take to artifacts we encounter in museums.

What does this reveal about cultural practice and perspective?

How did context inform the creation of this artifact?

What does this artifact say about being human? A human of a certain age, size, race, in a certain place in time?

Our Own Notes

In *Pedagogical Documentation in Early Childhood*, Susan Stacey (2015) encourages educators to document with an attitude of experimentation: rough documentation, documentation that shares short stories and chronicles the trajectories of brief explorations (as opposed to large, lengthy panels), and other small moments that make up the days. She insists that documentation does not always need to be typed, well-written, or otherwise public-facing. Documentation, she invites us to see, is a process, valuable in itself.

Robert Emerson, Rachel Fretz, and Linda Shaw (2011, 23), in *Writing Ethnographic Field Notes*, call writing notes "writing, participating, observing as a means of understanding another way of life." The jottings that are the fruit of our in-the-moment reflections on what is unfolding before us closely mirror what Stacey (2015) refers to as *rough documentation*—written on note cards or scraps of paper—the little ideas that float around. This rough documentation is, as Emerson and colleagues (2011, 29) note, "brief written records" that capture the essence of the events using "key words and phrases."

In what many consider to be the seminal work on the Reggio approach, Carolyn Edwards and colleagues insist that educators, in their "pay[ing of] close attention to the children," ought to describe their observations of the children and themselves in ways that, while idiosyncratic, are also "understandable to others and able to be communicated [within discussions]" (2012, 155). In other words, one's field notes and jottings ought to be suffused with a reflexive hue that is not afraid or hesitant to turn our gaze back toward ourselves. This reflexivity also includes a firm understanding of one's own positionality.

Documentation and ethnography invite us to consider our positionality, to not write ourselves out of narratives that we recount, and to consider how what we say is informed by our experiences and ideas and the intersections of the way we are in the world, including what we've studied. While we touched on this in chapter 3, it bears repeating here insofar as it's always good to be reminded that we are operating from our own individual perspectives, vision, and ideas of humanity, of childhood, and of what it means to be a small human and to be a big human interacting with small humans.

Uncovering, Confirming, and Creating Meaning through Dialogue and Children's Reflections

Gathering children's insights into their own experiences is important so that we do justice to the reflexive nature of documentation. Documentation, in this conceptualization, is a living artifact that serves as the physical manifestation of a conversation we are having about images of childhood. Documentation itself can also be the catalyst for such conversations. In qualitative research, a similar construct called *respondent validation* describes this dialogue. Respondents affirm or challenge the inferences that a researcher makes about a process or event they have observed or participated in. In this act of discussing, the researcher and respondents can uncover or create new meanings.

When we invite children to offer their reflections, we communicate to them that we care about what they have to say in matters that pertain to their lives. We are in line with article 12 of the United Nations Convention on the Rights of the Child (2009). And maybe we are surprised at what the children have to teach us!

Within, Outside, and Beyond Time

Ethnographies of childhood by scholars such as Johanna Einarsdottir and William Corsaro and educators such as Vivian Paley and Jane Katch often take place over years across multiple settings. Usually these authors center on a particular phenomenon over the course of many years—whether it's play, storytelling, artistic creation, or relational development. Each instance of a similar occurrence across time, each repeated, extended observation and encounter, reveals new layers of a common experience and allows the adult wondering at the lives of the children under their consideration to speak in new, interesting ways about their work.

While this may appear daunting at first glance, what is working with a young child if not the decision and commitment to repeatedly embrace familiarity as if it were new? At its heart, this repeated encounter is analogous to teaching: taking the mundane and making it strange, understanding how this phenomenon that you have seen a thousand times before is unique and, at the same time, in conversation with a thousand other similar moments.

These experiences and perspectives, gathered over time, give us the context necessary to be able to see and speak about patterns in children's lives with sensitivity. Therefore, as we consider what this perspective can lend to us in our work with young children, we can take heart with the knowledge that whether our observations and the experiences we gather are appreciated in the moment, they are all contributing to a valuable store of knowledge that will inform our—and likely, others'—ways of seeing children, interacting with them, and conceptualizing the work they do.

ETHNOGRAPHIC DOCUMENTATION IN THE SERVICE OF CHILDREN'S LIVES

As we conclude this chapter, it is helpful for us to consider what the goal is. After all, we have considered a broad array of practices that, if we fail to remind ourselves of our motivations, run the risk of eclipsing the main idea. Let me be clear: I am working from a particular aesthetic and philosophical lens, and my ends are not, at least in writing this book, neutral. I believe, and strongly, that documenting children's lives with this lens (which I believe accords their lives the respect they deserve) also positions us to advocate for their lives in spheres where the everyday experiences such as play, open-ended exploration, and the value inherent in the in-between moments—transitions, mealtimes, lingerings, fleeting moments in the hallway—are at risk of being overlooked or devalued.

Ritchie (2019, 14) writes that ethnography "offer[s] pathways toward greater awareness of and insights into the lives of people in the communities of focus." How, through understanding the connections between ethnography and documentation practice, do we build a deeper appreciation for the lives of those in our care and with whom we come into contact? Ritchie adds that ethnography can be seen as "a way of listening and a way of hearing, since it provides a means of giving voice to the concerns of young children, their families, communities, and teachers in diverse settings" (14).

We might wonder where and in what ways has our ability to hear what children say, to listen to what children are communicating, shifted to become more robust or powerful? Where have we, because of our listening, tuned into the concerns of young children and their communities of care?

Thus far we have reflected on our images of children and childhood, established that we have unique positions of privileged proximity to children's lives and experiences, and considered how documentation and ethnography draw upon similar if not the same dispositions, realizing that an ethnographic lens helps us ask new questions that extend beyond the confines of our curricular goals as traditionally conceived. This ethnographic lens invites us to ask new and different questions that extend beyond the typical questions of content and mechanics (despite the import these retain).

As we move forward, we will consider how all of these, taken together, allow us to speak in a different way—and that the way we can speak gives us important tools as we work toward advocating for an appreciation and celebration of children's everyday lives that extends far beyond curricular goals or other adult ends.

Reflections

What are your current practices of documentation in the classroom? What sort of framing do you use? What are you interested in documenting? What are you required to document?

In what ways are you already incorporating elements of an ethnographic lens or frame in your documentation?

What is a phenomenon that you don't typically think much about during the day—something that you take for granted as boring or uninteresting? I invite you to attempt to document this through an ethnographic lens. What is happening? What does it mean? How do the children behave during it? What do they think about the phenomenon itself?

If you were to document this unremarkable phenomenon over the course of many days, what patterns might emerge? If you do document it, what do you notice? Might anything you are seeing have something to teach adults about what it means to be a child broadly? What it means to be a child in your classroom?

Chapter 5

Advocating for Children's Lives

INTRODUCTION: EMBRACING THE POSSIBILITIES OF PROXIMATE GAZE

At this point, we've considered how our images of children and childhood are enhanced by documenting and attending to children's lives in ways that integrate elements of traditional documentation and ethnography. Our unique and privileged proximity to children means that we have both an opportunity and an obligation to ensure that the environments within which they spend their days are responsive to and supportive of their needs, abilities, and competencies. However, the fact remains that no setting is perfect, whether we are working in open-ended, child-directed contexts or more traditionally minded spaces, Montessori-, Waldorf-, or Reggio-inspired contexts, nature-based or indoor settings. Sooner or later we will find ourselves in a position where we feel compelled to advocate to families, to our institutions, to our colleagues—and even, perhaps, to ourselves— for children's rights to live their lives engaged in meaningful play, deep inquiry, and self-directedness. Therefore, we turn our lens to advocacy. In this chapter, I outline multiple examples of how a highly attuned, ethnographic lens for capturing children's experiences contributes to an advocacy rooted in a personal relationship with children at the peer-group, classroom, and institutional levels.

I begin by telling the story of the Rough Boys, a group of pre-K friends who enjoyed rough play and needed some support to continue it safely. Using an ethnographic lens with this group of children helped me to reframe rough play—instead of existing as a distraction, it became a cultural practice that I needed to understand. With my new understanding of the children's practice and goals, I strove to help them do it safely and, at the same time, invite the administration to view the practice differently. After, I explore ways that using this ethnographic lens enabled me to view the tasks of daily life and relationship as essential curriculum in a context that, despite its purported child centeredness, often failed to consider children's priorities in its explicit framing of the curriculum. Following this, I take a look at tree climbing, which is a classroom practice in our nature-based preschool. I explore how viewing climbing as more than a gross-motor activity and as an engine of relationship and a catalyst for the development of peer cultural practices both strengthened my own regard for the practice and helped me articulate its value to curious passersby in a public park.

In the final case study, I explore the ways that documenting children's experiences through an ethnographic lens was useful in creating a framework for translating the practices of our nature-based preschool for parents, families, and community members. I also touch upon how this framework guided our classroom as we transitioned from a fully outdoor context to a hybrid model that moved between indoor urban spaces and outdoor public parks.

~

ADVOCACY AS RELATIONSHIP

As we begin this chapter, it will be valuable to define *advocacy*. In the dictionary, advocacy is defined as "public support for or recommendation of a particular cause or policy." Advocacy is the outward manifestation of an inner devotion to or conviction about a cause. In this case, we are talking about the rights of children.

When I asked my close colleague Clare Loughran, MEd, founder of NOLA Nature School in New Orleans, Louisiana, about what she thinks *advocacy* means in relation to the work of early childhood educators, she had this to say:

> *For those of us who are close to children, advocacy involves seeing children, what they need, and what is unfolding, and pushing forward ideas and legislation that enables children to thrive. As educators and administrators in early childhood programs, we see firsthand the importance of play in children's lives. It is our job to protect the joy and fun of learning through play. We must help others see and understand the value of play. We advocate for a child's right to joyful learning.*

Advocacy is also closely tied to relationship—indeed, it is the result of deep relationships. In knowing children and documenting and following their lives closely, we often come to love them. The love we have for children builds on and motivates us to know them more, and this motivation combines with our intuitive and professional awareness of children's interests, needs, and areas for growth. All of this established, we are then impelled to speak out when we see children, their needs, their interests, and their capacities, being dismissed, disregarded, or downplayed.

Advocacy can be something like a small act of resistance in the face of a set of norms or ideas that are contrary to our convictions. This might, for example, look like reminding a colleague, with all gentleness, of a developmentally appropriate early literacy practice if we see them insisting that children engage with letters, words, and stories in ways for which they are not ready.

Advocacy can also involve an active contribution—whether to a body of thought or repertoire of practice—that highlights something that we are convinced is valuable or meaningful in a child's life. It can support something that we want to see continue to happen in children's lives, such as increasing the time we spend outdoors or enshrining activities that integrate art as part of curriculum.

Whatever its nature, at its core, advocacy is about relationship. It says that I will stick up for you. I will vouch for you. I will support you. It also asserts, after each of these, that I am willing to endure the tension that comes from resisting those who do not. I am willing, it says again, to feel uncomfortable in doing what I can to make sure that you have as much physical, psychological, and social space as possible to thrive.

As adults who listen to children, who care for children, who wish to support children in their explorations of the world as they construct self and community, we are inextricably linked to children. Our relationships with children involve respect and positive regard, inspiring us to seek the ideal conditions for their intellectual and creative development.

CASE 1: THE ROUGH BOYS

It was an interesting year, to say the least. I had signed on to teach kindergarten (at the same school I had attended for elementary myself) in a loosely defined, full-time role. Within six weeks the arrangement was evidently not working, and I was asked to cover a maternity leave for a teacher in pre-K. I instantly gelled with the children and lead teacher and quickly settled into a natural-feeling rhythm. About as quickly, it became clear to me that some of the children in the class were exploring rough-and-tumble play in ways that started off friendly but oftentimes ended in an all-out brawl. Engaging in rough-and-tumble play is developmentally appropriate, but hurting classmates and friends in anger reinforces unhelpful and potentially damaging (socially and physically) norms. Of course something had to be done—but what?

The children at play on the playground.

Two children right before a wrestle.

For my colleagues, the answer was simple. The play needed to stop.

Unsurprisingly, the teachers' insistence did nothing. It rarely (if ever!) does in these cases.

I decided to adopt a different approach. After all, as a new teacher I had little to lose—I knew that within half a year I'd be on to a different classroom. More importantly, I was curious about what the children were doing, and I believed I could see the genuine enjoyment they took in this play. I wanted to know more.

However, it feels important to say that I was not curious about *why* this practice was occurring (rough-and-tumble play is both common and well documented). Neither was I curious about how to stop it (this would prove, in my estimation, a fruitless endeavor). Instead, I wanted to know *how the children interpreted the practice*. What would listening to their own voices, words, and experiences reveal? A quick search on how to talk to children about rough play brought me to Jane Katch's (2001) *Under Deadman's Skin: Discovering the Meaning of Children's Violent Play*, and her respect for and inquiry into children's violent behavior became the catalyst for my inquiry into children's rough-and-tumble play.

I was also inspired by a view of children as creators of and participants in cultures that differ from adults. I wanted to consider the perspectives of the primary participants in this cultural practice. Perhaps these would yield insights that would challenge my colleagues' and my own preexisting notions about rough play. Perhaps this would help us develop tools for responding to this behavior in a way that met our adult desire for group harmony while also respecting the desires and instincts of the children.

And so I decided to do something different. I decided to take photographs.

My reflective journal notes read:

Instead of stopping rough play each time it occurred or each time a child complained (which, at one time, became nearly once every couple of minutes), I began turning the boys away and, instead, responded to their tattling by taking photos using my phone or the classroom iPad. I would stand nearby, always watching and never interfering. When they would touch, tackle, push, or punch, I'd do what I could to get a photo of the incident or of its immediate aftermath.

And, immediately after:

At best, it seemed as if nothing happened. The boys, if anything, were more empowered by my permission to continue their play.

Rooted in Observation

Fully aware of the uniqueness of my privileged access to these moments (after all, children are usually discouraged from this sort of play in public and even in many classrooms), and as an educator who is also interested in taking an ethnographic approach to children, I felt a need to observe first. Ethnographers are observers. As I observed, I remained aware of my positionality as a schoolteacher—if a situation became seriously dangerous, I had both a moral and professional obligation to intervene.

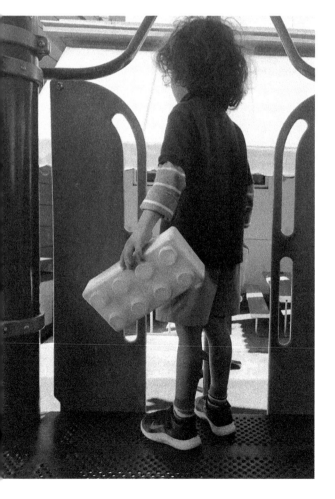

Keeping watch from the top of the play structure, holding the block just in case it needs to be used in self-defense. For those wondering, the block does not end up needing to be thrown.

The slide was a particularly exciting place to get rough. Here one child holds on to the play structure while the other child (whose feet are visible) attempts to pass them on the slide by climbing over their body.

Most often no intervention was necessary. In addition, I like to imagine that my tendency to observe the children without intervention deepened our trust. Nonetheless, I was also vividly aware of my power relative to the children. I had something less than the full authority of the lead teacher but much more than a child or peer. Every educator interested in work of this sort, especially when examining a practice such as rough-and-tumble play, has to be ready to navigate the line between being a trusted adult and an obligated protector. The children knew that barring serious danger they would be free to continue their play—and likely trusted me both to allow it and to protect them throughout it. For a while, my physical presence seemed to be enough—the boys trusted me to protect and respect their play and to keep them safe. That is, until—as inevitably happens—something changed.

The Turning Point

Two boys were tumbling on the turf near the slide.

Clearly, with the slightest tinge of what I detected as urgency, a cry: "Stop!" Caught up in the emotions of the moment, one child ignored the other's protests.

"Stop!" resonated a little louder, but before my strides could bring me to the two embroiled children, one had already pushed the other down. To make matters worse, the child who had protested scraped his shin, and a single droplet of bright-red blood rose to the surface. The tears came instantly, quickly followed by my own frustration and even anger.

While objectively a minor injury, in retrospect I can see how the cut and blood served as a visible symbol of the trust that was, in this case, broken. I had not kept the children safe, the children had not kept one another feeling good or safe, and now a child had an injury to go along with a story of being pushed by a peer.

A series of events followed: a conversation between the head of the Lower School and the child, then the notification of the children's families. To my eye, both attempts at amelioration centered on punitive measures and shame. While I understood that it was not okay to harm friends and violate bodily autonomy, this felt like a gross oversimplification of children's intentions. It also read to me like a failure to support children in wrestling with the nuances of their play. It did, however, stop the play temporarily.

Despite my frustration, I also wondered if my project was too ambitious and if treating the children's rough-and-tumble play as a cultural practice that deserved to be respected, unpacked, and tailored to serve the interests of its participants while adhering to the stated goals of the institution was doomed to fail.

I didn't give up. But I knew I needed more to share with my colleagues before making a new case.

Investigating the Nuances of a Cultural Practice

Some days later, my optimism apparently resurged. I invited the children involved in the aforementioned incident into the hallway for a conversation. This was the start of nearly five months over which we had nearly a dozen conversations about rough play. Often these conversations were grounded in photographs of actual events that took place. We began to speak about what was going on—imperfectly on my part, as you will see—but we spoke nonetheless.

A snapshot from our first conversation in the hallway. Wayne and Martin look at the photographs.

Field Notes, November 16, 2018

We are sitting in the hallway during open-ended playtime in the classroom. Wayne, Tyler, Oliver, and Manny are outside with me. I chose to find my way out of the classroom to invite them to focus but in retrospect wonder if it felt punitive. The boys, however, are willing to sit, speak, and share with me.

I begin recording. The audio reveals some shuffling sounds as I move my phone to a place where it is both inconspicuous and also able to pick up the sounds of our voices.

"What can we do to make sure our friends feel good, always?" I wonder aloud.

"Give them an ice pack," one child suggests. I cannot tell if he is serious or attempting humor.

"But what about when their inside is hurting, their heart is hurting?" I say, offering what I intend as a clarification.

"That's what my mommy does to me," he finished.

"What does she do to you?"

"Uhh, put, put like an ice pack on your skin." Tyler clarifies his peer's meaning to me.

I invite Oliver to share. He also suggests an ice pack.

Why, I wonder, is it not clear to them? I do not recall feeling frustrated, but I hear a tinge of seriousness creep into my voice—an urgency of my own.

"If you're crying because someone hurts your feelings, does an ice pack help?"

If they do not show me that they get it, then how will I convince others that they really do? Do they?

"No," the reply comes.

"No, it doesn't," I say.

Listening back, I can hear how this didn't leave full space for the children to answer or respond. After all, no work of ethnography is perfect or free from bias, but to get to children's understanding we must be willing to fumble, fail, and fumble again.

The conversation continued on. The audio reveals that in response to my question, Manny added that if someone was hurting we could show them affection.

"Give them some love," he shared.

Next, a friend added, "Share a funny joke."

Immediately, Oliver tells one: "Why does Pete the cat walking down the street?" he starts. A beat.

"Because he wanted to play hide-and-seek!"

At this, we all ended what began feeling like a very serious conversation in a fit of giggles. Within a couple of minutes, the children were back on the playground and I along with them. While we finished our initial session telling jokes, the stage was set for our future discussions, deconstructions, and re- and co-constructed knowledges to emerge.

Sometime later the boys and I were looking at another photo set. In the series, the boys are playing on the slide, one's body is halfway in and halfway out of the slide.

Wayne and Oliver take a close look at a photograph.

Martin offers the first comments: "Oliver said, 'I'll save you Martin!' and I said, 'Okay, Oliver!'"

Wayne interjects, "Yeah, but—"

Martin, however, continues. The two are now speaking at the same time. I remind Martin that it is Wayne's turn to speak.

"But um," Wayne begins, ". . . but um Oliver pulled me to the side, and I really didn't like that."

"And now it's Oliver's turn to talk," I add.

"And I was, I was—um, because I was worried that Martin would get hurt, um, 'cause they were wrestling."

The *process* of constructing what this play meant *to the children* was the goal of our discussion. The children revealed threads of enjoyment, evident in Martin's sharing, but there was also dislike, even fear. The positive and the negative are not mutually exclusive, and we do not strive to oversimplify the experience of play. Children are more than capable of making decisions, reflecting on those decisions through multiple lenses, and grappling with the consequences of those decisions. They can understand nuance—that joy, fear, and concern all exist in a constellation alongside one another. Rather than seeking to eliminate any one of those feelings, sensations, or emotions, there is value in helping children navigate, manage, and understand them.

We are sitting together again, sometime in the spring, and I ask the boys to tell me about a photo set.

"We're wrestling, since Mateo started it. I just wanted to join," Walter begins. A desire for connection, to be with and play with a friend.

"I was getting stepped on by Mateo," Oliver adds. A bit of discomfort, perhaps?

"It doesn't look like you're crying here," I note.

Oliver replies, "I wasn't—it didn't hurt that much." Discomfort, some pain, but not enough that it outweighs or overpowers the ability to enjoy the fruits of connection. Do not children, we can wonder, deserve the right to determine this boundary?

As I reflect on these conversations, the question of what might have happened if we had not explored these topics together continually recurs. What would it have said to the children if I, like their other teachers, had begun to police their play? Although I will never know for sure, I like to think that, at the very least, these conversations allowed the children to make connections between their own experiences over time and to reflect on what it might look like to notice friends' discomfort, respond in a friendly way, and discuss what it means to care and be cared for.

Expanding the Chorus of Voices

As educators, we can take inspiration from researchers, particularly those who inquire into the ways that a single set of behaviors or practices is perceived across multiple societies and their various social contexts. For educators, this would mean taking an episode of play and asking those who were not involved to offer their commentaries about it. These others could be from within the same class where the play unfolded, or they might be from other classes or even other schools. If one asks children in the same class but who were not involved, for example, they might learn things about who is friends with whom or about other aspects of the relationships between the children featured in the episode that they might not have otherwise known. If an educator takes the scenario outside of the classroom or school context, they might find that children in other peer communities have feelings that differ (intensely or in small ways). Upon further investigation, they might also learn ways the children's views about play relate to the influence of teachers in those classrooms, or even how children's judgments are related to particular elements of their peer culture, and so on. There are, I am attempting to highlight, multiple possibilities for how a single episode of play can be informative about the context it is embedded in and even beyond its context. You might even observe differences in children's views along traditional gender lines. Bringing the phenomena we observe and document to children beyond the group featured in the documentation is a meaningful way to contextualize what a particular peer group's cultural practice might mean for a broader community of children. There may be broad consensus, or there might be interesting variability in opinion. We will not know unless we invite the perspectives of the experts—the children.

The Teachers' Response

At the close of the year, I gathered my documentation together and compiled what I believed was a compelling report of the children's interest in and capacity to reflectively engage in rough play. I detailed the conversations I'd had with the Rough Boys, shared the photographs and the philosophical underpinnings—and yet it wasn't enough. Ultimately, the teachers in this school decided that they were still uncomfortable with the children roughhousing. While I may have chosen a different course of action, this is not something on which I will offer a value judgment. And this is the hard truth—advocacy doesn't always lead to instant or immediate transformation.

I share this outcome first because it is the reality—very often our advocacy, however compellingly presented, will come up against norms and institutions over which we have little (or only transient and fleeting) influence. We are members of dynamic ecosystems that shift and change constantly—directors come and go, teachers come and go, children and families come and go. However, we need not be deterred. After all, we are in the long game—investing in outcomes we will never see. I like to think that in some years, someone will look back and wonder, even if only for a second, about what it means when they see another group of rough boys, rough girls, or rough children rolling around on the ground. I hope when play eventually stops, they will pause, ask the children's thoughts, and realize that there is nuance and intention behind the behavior they are observing. This would mean that a new image of the child is starting to take place, an image that takes time and experience to develop. And for me that would feel like a win.

Lessons from the Rough Boys

As we sit with the Rough Boys, we revisit each of the principles outlined in the previous chapters.

Image of Children and Childhood

The story of the Rough Boys is an example of what it might look like if we accept the reality that children, as complex beings, have thoughts and feelings that shift and change and if out of respect for children's agency and humanity we challenge ourselves to accept this. Sometimes the boys wanted to play rough, and other times they didn't want to play rough. They somewhat understood the potential implications of their actions (that they might get hurt) but on some levels did not. However, the entire way through, they wrestled admirably with their conflicting feelings much in the same way that all humans assess the risk involved with daily activities.

Inexhaustible Richness

In this work, I choose to see rough-and-tumble play as full of opportunities to learn more about children, their lives, their thinking, and so on. This means that, far from only viewing rough-and-tumble play as an opportunity to teach children about the things valued in the official curriculum (getting a teacher when things get rough, choosing another sort of game to play, and so on), I strove to see what else there might be to learn.

Unique Positioning

My proximity to children also meant that I was able to look closely at the play—that I was looking at the play not only when conflict arose but also during the challengingly joyful moments. Through this proximity, my understanding of the children's feelings and my thinking about what they might be relishing within this play was able to be informed and influenced by the children themselves rather than entirely by my own preconceptions.

Documentation as Ethnography

Framing rough play as a cultural practice and the children as a group with its own evolutionary trajectory helped me tint the language I used to speak about this work with others. It also helped underscore that there might be things to learn from this practice, if only we were willing to sustainedly look directly at the things that at first glance may have seemed strange or made us uncomfortable.

Advocating for Children's Lives

By documenting this play using this lens, I sought to advocate for children and invite my fellow educators to consider how they might create space for rough-and-tumble play in their daily classroom practices. While my advocacy was, at least during my tenure in this space, unsuccessful in enacting formal policy-level change on a grade or administrative level—the roughhousing was, ultimately, quashed—I like to think that the children who participated in these discussions felt seen and honored.

CASE 2: A CURRICULUM OF LIVED EXPERIENCE

In many schools, there is, perhaps, an ideal way of being, of teaching, of working with children, of having a classroom. Every institution has its own ideal. This ideal, or some close approximation, is often what is presented to prospective families and caregivers who are considering enrolling their children in our programs. As educators, however, we know that this ideal is typically far from the reality of what happens each day within a given classroom. This is not to say that what happens in classrooms is subpar, inappropriate, or otherwise inadequate—on the contrary. Our proximity allows us to see how each group of children is different and to know that this variability means that, even when institutional ideals and expectations remain static, every classroom is different every year as we encounter different people, different young humans whose ways of being interact with one another in new ways to create an environment that is itself wholly new. An ethnographic lens gives us a perspective through which to capture the relational, contextual, and specific aspects of these new environments.

Setting and Context: The Preschool

Some years ago, I taught at a preschool that explicitly espoused a philosophy that centered co-constructivist project work (where children are considered active participants in generating and directing curriculum alongside educators). In truth, however, the preschool was in a period of transition between directors and between its founding philosophies and those of the new guard of educators. As part of a larger school, we were also increasingly in conversation with—and facing implicit pressure and collegial tension with—educators who would be receiving many of the children into their pre-K and kindergarten classrooms the following year. All of this meant that although our school billed itself as constructivist, in practice each educator's classroom was its own world. Teachers, wherever they are, tend to bring their own favorite philosophies to bear in the work they do in the classroom, regardless of the overarching ideal. Some teachers were inspired by the Project Approach and Creative Curriculum, others strove to adhere to the principles of the Reggio approach, while still others were more or less wedded to traditional didactic styles in efforts to get children "ready" for pre-K. While I existed in my own world to the extent that I was able, I often found myself beholden to expectations tied to the school's philosophy that meant managing children's movements, inquiries, and schedules in ways that genuinely felt—and my coteacher that year agreed—developmentally inappropriate.

I was part of a system, one that is not uncommon in early childhood spaces, that desired two realities that were difficult to reconcile. So what did we do? How did taking an ethnographic lens to children's lives give us the language, tools, and perspective to push back against these restrictive norms?

Documentation of Daily Doings as Advocacy

One of the purposes of documentation as it is dominantly conceived is accountability—to prove that we are doing work with the children that aligns with our program's standards. Indeed, popular phrases such as "making learning visible," with all its respectful connotations, are just other ways of saying, "You have to prove that what you are doing is giving children the skills that society says they need in the way society says you should."

However, a variety of research shows us that for two year olds turning three, the primary curriculum is social and emotional. Children are learning how to *be,* how to be *at school* and how to be *at school with one another*, and every day is a significant lesson in its very unfolding. For our school, it was also important to show that there was a consistency of vision informing the daily goings-on and between classrooms and to show that each classroom contributed to developmental milestones for two- and three-year-olds on multiple levels.

Therefore, I decided to document the children's work in a different way. Rather than focusing on particular projects, such as gardening, exploring emotions, or exploring paint—all of which were part of our emergent curricula that year—I decided to document the minutiae of the day. By using the forms of documentation to study the bits and pieces of everyday life, I constructed what read to me like brief ethnographic snapshots of our classroom culture. I invited families and administrators to take a new lens to the basic activities of our days—those that, for very young children, tend to take up the most space.

In the next sections, I explore a few examples of how our curriculum of lived experience supported our classroom in meeting the needs of the children in our care and how it developed and deepened a new regard among children's adults for the basic processes that comprise a child's day. Overall, these periodic displays of documentation sought to show how in the daily doings of life in classroom community together we were embarking upon a project of connection—to one another, to our peers, and to the natural spaces and world in which we found ourselves.

WALKING: A RITUAL OF COMMUNITY AND PERSONAL CONNECTION

One of the most basic processes that made up our days was walking. As anyone who has worked with a group of young children knows, walking together as a group, in any configuration, is a significant event. Not only does walking often indicate a transition from one activity to another, but it also intersects and overlaps with other aspects of children's lives and experiences in ways that have significant consequences for how it ultimately unfolds. A child's response to an impending walk and comportment throughout that walk is very different, for example, if the child is walking to or away from something that they find desirable, if the walking is interrupting play or an emotional challenge, if they have eaten recently or not, if they are wet—from any number of liquids—sniffly, coughing, giddy, or what have you.

Walking is meaningful, and, I argued, constituted a curriculum within itself. It was representative of children's connection.

Setting out for a long walk!

At our preschool, though we are located in a little annex, we are also part of a larger world—the Big School—that exists just across the football field. For many of the children, the Big School is more than just a physical reality; it is a personal one as well. Many of their parents and family members attend or have attended, or currently or formerly worked there, and many of them, surely, will spend a great deal of their lives there. Therefore, the walk to and around the Big School serves as so much more than a pleasant gross-motor activity or diversion (though it is those as well). Indeed, it is a way to connect with the culture of the children's families and histories, as well as to forge an appreciation of the broader institution of which [our preschool] is an indispensable part.

By taking this basic practice of walking through campus and making it strange again, by shifting the frame from basic activity to cultural phenomenon, we were able to wonder what was happening underneath the surface. By parsing it and reflecting on the ways it was in conversation with our broader curricular goals (community, the development of regulation, the formation of social relationships, and more), we were able to develop a lexicon through which we could with increasing confidence express, in the terms required of us by our institution, how this seeming aberration—spending an entire afternoon on a walk—was actually perfectly in line with its stated goals.

Carrying a long pole on a walk.

MEANINGFUL MESSES: REFRAMING OUTCOME AS INTENTION

Making messes is an inevitable component of early childhood life. However, for young children, the making and the cleaning up of messes is an extended opportunity for meaning-making and experimenting with and trying on roles, building efficacy, and more. Rather than emphasize how children were learning to keep things clean or orderly (valuable yet adult priorities), it felt important to me to highlight the intentionality that suffused the process of making and cleaning up messes.

In our room, we had a sensory table that, for some weeks, was filled with play sand. Sand, of course, eludes easy capture and containment. When indoors, sand also has the remarkable capacity to find its way *everywhere*. On the day in question, the sand was scattered around the sensory table and its environs in ways that resembled a snowdrift.

My initial instinct, my typical instinct, would have been to clean up the sand and imagine a way to make it so that it didn't leave the table next time, let alone spill over into adjacent areas of the room. However, on this day, I waited and decided to take pictures instead.

Working together to clean up the spilled sand.

Back into the table it goes!

Before long Jacques, just shy of three years old, with a sunny disposition and an iconic bowl cut, walked over to the table. Jacques was never one to shy away from a hearty task, and within seconds he had grabbed a broom and dustpan and begun sweeping up the sand. He was focused, intentional, and methodical.

In short order, two other classmates began to sweep as well. Patrick grabbed two dustpans—one in each hand—and Leah retrieved a broom from the bathroom and began to sweep sand into them as well. Once Jacques and Leah finished their work, Henry joined Patrick, taking up the handheld broom relinquished by Jacques.

In writing up the documentation for this occasion, I wanted to be sure to invite the adults reading it to move beyond considerations of how, in taking up brooms and dustpans, children were "learning to clean up their messes." Instead, it seemed valuable to wonder at *the mess itself*. What if mess is reconstrued as a *child-created circumstance* rather than as an unwelcome side effect of children's explorations? Yes, the cleanup was meaningful; yes, the social and cooperative skills the children worked on through cleaning up this mess were meaningful. But what if we understood that the creation of the mess holds deep meaning and value as well? How might a child's frivolity and joy in making a mess also be coupled with an implicit awareness that, following the bit of chaos they enact, there is an opportunity to clean it up? What if a child knows this and wishes it to happen?

Making the paradigm of mess-making and mess-cleaning strange involved, in this instance, framing the cleanup process—familiar to the audience of adults—as a result of the children's agency in freely making and moving through a messy environment. This meant waiting, watching, observing. It meant documenting the mundane—born from the belief that the smallest moments, like a messy morning at the sand table, hold deep meaning. It also provided a small opportunity to reframe and reorient the conversations within our community of families and educators. As you reflect on your work, I invite you to think about some of the following:

Are there any small practices within your classroom that you might begin to explore with a new lens?

What spaces, activities, or regular occurrences might you make strange?

How might you share your reframings with the broader community?

SITTING AT A LITTLE TABLE: TRANSFORMING A PHYSICAL OBJECT INTO RELATIONSHIPS

The Little Table was a square table in that natural finish so in vogue in many early childhood spaces that toes the line between bland and calming. It was also, as the moniker suggests, little, with just enough room for four snuggly gathered small children. Yes, even the mere act of sitting at a table is valuable, a rich, meaningful experience.

In our documentation, however, we did not come right out and say this. In contrast to the above, we primarily framed the Little Table as a space in the service of cognitive ends—cultivating focus, scaffolding perspective-taking, facilitating collaboration. In this instance, advocating for children's lives meant using language that was common within the dominant framework of our center so we could subvert it, so as to ensure that children's experiences were honored. We must be translators between the worlds of children and the worlds of adults. Documenting children's explorations at the Little Table is an example of what it might look like to play both sides of the coin, if you will. It shows how we can use dominant linguistic forms to give children access to the experiences that allow them to fulfill the ends that, due to our proximity, we see they care most about.

Hanging out at the Little Table.

The story of the Little Table was also gathered across time. Through photographs a story emerged that suggested that for the children there was a deeper relational element at play in their dealings with this Little Table. It was a space where they could sit with family members to eat breakfast before saying goodbyes, a space where they could enjoy snack and lunch in the company of one or two special friends, a place to sit just because. The Little Table also became a social crossroads where children who were not regularly part of one another's primary social groups would connect and collaborate over mutual interests.

SHARING IDEAS: CHILDREN TAKING CONTROL OF A CLASSROOM RITUAL

In my very first year of teaching, my mentor teacher introduced me to the concept of show-and-tell for preschoolers. Over the course of our time together, I watched as young children showed with great pride items they brought from home, bringing pieces of their lives into the classroom on a weekly basis.

Two years later, in a new school, I strove to implement a similar practice that began as a carbon copy of my previous experiences. The children would come to school and place their "share" (the object they intended to show the class) in a basket at the start of the day. At the close of morning play, shares were put up out of reach on a high shelf, and then at a group meeting time, a teacher would randomly draw an item from the basket, and the child whose item it was would step forward, share, and take any questions or comments from the group.

However, the children in this class had a different vision of this ritual. Their interest in share time was so great that instead of bringing shares in on our specified share day, they began bringing them in on multiple days. Often, if children did not have or forgot a share, they would take an object from their cubbie, such as an extra shirt or even spare pair of undies, to share. Before long, share time became a daily event.

As time went on, the children began to feature different artifacts. No longer were shares comprised mainly of favorite stuffed animals, trucks, dolls, balls, and the like. By the halfway point of the year, the children began to steadily integrate their representations—works of art, sculpture, and movement—into their rotation of sharing. The cultural ritual had evolved, the normative practices of the children's peer culture having made space for more expansive notions of sharing.

One photograph reveals a child, two years and ten months old, holding up a standard letter-sized sheet of paper. Her classmates are seated in a circle around her.

"I made a big, big, big [Big School]!" she proudly declared.

My coteacher and I interpreted this shift as a signal that sharing time had transitioned from being primarily about thinking about objects from home to being an occasion for sharing creativity within the community. This ritual itself, while not a formal piece of the curriculum espoused by our school (or at least not the primary component celebrated by the dominant discourse), was a key part of the children's processes of making meaning within their daily lives. It was also, a close look and ethnographic lens revealed, completely in line with the goals of our curriculum.

Lessons from a Curriculum of Lived Experience

✦ Image of Children and Childhood

While our center had a strong image of children as capable, competent, agentic, creative, and deserving of space to play and inquire in intellectual and social safety, we were beholden to certain expectations and norms that challenged or contradicted these realities. We were expected, for example, to have extensive lesson plans and were often encouraged to enact norms in the name of classroom management that felt overly restrictive. However, as educators working with children who are dedicated to looking at their lives up close, we were committed to engaging with this tension, which for us looked like finding ways to free up space for children to play and explore in ways that respected their autonomy, interests, and development.

✦ Inexhaustible Richness

Viewing moments as ripe with meaning was also a key contributor to our ability to and interest in documenting the children's lives as we did. Mess-making and sweeping (child directed and not merely teacher inspired) were meaningful. Children's "shares," and their desire to share, were more than just childhood enthusiasm—they represented the children's willful appropriation and transformation of an adult-originated ritual. And, within the appropriation and transformation, the children began to direct the ritual to their desired end, slowly shifting its emphasis from adult-produced artifacts to child-created ones. Rather than cast it aside, we interpreted this shift as meaningfully communicative about children's understandings of this ritual.

✦ Unique Positioning

We understood that as educators it was our role to bear the onus of the double act of speaking to children's experiences and connecting them to institutional norms and needs while also, given our intimacy with children's daily lives, seeking to uncover how children's experiences even within those broader norms could and did shed light on what was most meaningful for them.

✦ Documentation as Ethnography

In each piece of our documentation, we strove to capture elements of children's experiences that went beyond the dominant curriculum. At times this meant using language that would be familiar to our administrators and families while also striving to find new and different ways of framing what we were seeing. Using an ethnographic lens allowed us to adopt a perspective from which to approach exploration of the everyday that makes us aware of the patterns, asynchronies, harmonies, and disfluencies that perpetually surround us.

✦✧ Advocating for Children's Lives

The most noticeable, and most important, outcome of this commitment to documenting the children's daily activities with this ethnographic lens was joy, and this joy in very short order deepened the relationships within our classroom community. Our center director appreciated the efforts that we made to chronicle children's lives, and families responded by expressing their enthusiasm for how this increased their children's desires to come to school and their own sense of connection to the classroom. In many ways, our insistence that we move past constraining norms that had not been serving our community likely contributed to this sense of well-being as well. Educators who are at ease in and confident that the work they are doing is both meaningful and fun are likely to transfer that ease to their children and beyond.

CASE 3: INVESTIGATING CHILDREN'S RIGHT TO CLIMB

During my time at NOLA Nature School, we operated in a highly visible public space—a public park adjacent to a shared playground, which featured walking paths and other public communal gathering spaces, including a café. This visibility and proximity to community was something we enjoyed. However, it also meant that onlookers often had (and shared with us) ideas about what children should be doing and how they should be in spaces. These ideas, especially those that expressed reservations about children's abilities to climb and their safety while climbing, contrasted with our school's philosophy, aims, and intentions. In this setting, as opposed to the prior settings, the administration supported children's expansive notions of climbing. And in these moments, facing doubt from the public, it felt important for the children and for us, as educators, to be able to present the work that was unfolding in terms that underscored its depth and value.

Moving Past Typical Notions of What Holds Worth: Beyond Gross-Motor Skills

When justifying climbing to others, we typically focus on the ways it builds on a wide array of physical and mental competencies, including risk assessment, gross- and fine-motor skills, and perspective-taking. At the same time, it is risky—there is an ever-present danger of falling, and the potential negative impacts of falling grow as children climb higher. However, my main interest in climbing involved neither of these realities. Instead, as the children in my class took more interest in climbing,

I felt that it was important to be able speak about this practice in ways that moved beyond the traditional adult-defined dimensions of value. The ethnographic lens was in the service of my own image of the child—the fruit of my own teacher inquiry.

I wanted to know why climbing held such appeal for children. What would their perspectives on climbing have to teach me about what and why climbing held such value as a cultural practice? To investigate this, I began to get up close and personal to climbing children, to observe them and to ask them about climbing, and to more intentionally document their behavior and words on this practice. Consider with me:

What do you think it might look like to shift from holding teachers accountable only to center-defined norms to norms that also consider children's priorities for their actions within the world?

I began with a mixture of observation and conversation. Given my daily proximity with the children, in short order these simple tools allowed me to move beyond typical surface-level descriptors of the climbing and why this practice held value. It also challenged me to think about what it could sound like to describe value through the justifications I gleaned from the children's work rather than my own.

Beyond Risk: Climbing and the Edge of Mortality

William looks out from the perfect vantage point.

I am spotting Ian and William. I have known both boys for a long time as they are well into their second year in my class. William is the oldest in the class at six years old, while Ian is fast approaching his fifth birthday. Despite his younger age, Ian is one of the two top climbers in the class. The following exchange reveals, perhaps, a glimpse into their ideas about climbing.

"When do you need a spotter? How do you know?" I ask them, aware that if anyone will have answers to this question, these two will. Ian answers sincerely.

"When we're scared." He is holding fast to a tree branch. Until that point, I have never heard Ian ask for help, but I now remember that he has always asked for a spotter before climbing.

Ever the leader, William chimes in: "Not when we're scared. When it's hard." For William, it appears, difficulty is the motivating factor. Or is it purely unfashionable to admit fear as a motivator?

This exchange, through a rich lens, also invites us to ask these questions:

In what ways and contexts is fear experienced?

Is it a result of feeling in physical danger? Of a lack of technical knowledge? Or the threat of physical danger as a result of the lack of technical knowledge?

How might the ways in which each of these children is expressing themselves reveal multiple sides to and layers of fear?

"It's not even hard," Laura, four years old and a highly experienced and highly skilled climber, adds matter-of-factly.

"When it's harder"—William forges forward—"like we might fall."

Yes, climbing is risk assessment, but climbing is also a way that this group of children wrestles with the boundaries of their own fear and ability—and vulnerability. Indeed, this reality is further confirmed when, later that day, Trey becomes frozen with fear at the top of a tree and struggles to make the descent.

The next day, I overhear a conversation between Laura and William.

"I don't wanna fall," Laura says. "I never fell in my whole life."

William wonders, "Ever do you care if you die?"

"Yes."

"How do you spell 'yes'?" William asks.

"Did you know you can die of hotness?" Laura asks.

"Actually, you can die of hotness, my mom told me," adds William.

Laura heads back down a branch.

William, Ian, and Louis move through branches in the forest.

I note that in the history of our class there have been some notable falls. I wonder if these two have been speaking about or have previously spoken about William's fall last year that resulted in a bloody nose, swollen eyes, and my class's final adventure to what had been called the Super Tree—a mighty fallen oak. Either way, limits, boundaries, and awareness of one's own limitations—and even one's own mortality—all seem to be aspects of this practice that children find valuable. Risk assessment is only the surface.

Being Able: Climbing as a Rite of Passage

Conversations between the children revealed that they also considered climbing a rite of passage. Through climbing, children demonstrated a competence and confidence that was, importantly, less contingent upon age and more on experience.

The day after Trey's difficult and emotional climb out of the tree, Griff is trying his hand at a climb. At three years old, he is among our youngest. He is also, however, among our most socially connected, and his motivation to maintain the leadership position he often enjoys in play, it seems, means he needs to be able to climb trees.

"Look Mr. Ron, I'm not scared!" I look his way and smile. He continues, "I even don't need no spotter. I'm even coming down. Nobody can't even catch me!" Griff is proud of himself. I wonder, might this be in light of Trey's very public difficulty the other day? Is Griff marking his physical and psychological distance from Trey through this declaration? Whom, exactly, is Griff reassuring?

Later that day, my field notes also record the following exchange between Trey and Griff.

"I used to be scared of every tree—but now I'm not! Now I'm four and I'm very strong!" Trey says

Griff looks at Trey.

"If you push me off, I'm going to fall off and die," Trey adds.

Griff laughs at that.

"No, I'm serious," Trey emphasizes.

"I'm serious too," Griff insists. "I don't want Trey to die."

Again, this awareness of and desire for one's own progress in climbing ability is evident. As I read them at least, these conversations reveal the children's striving to achieve what they saw as a rite of passage. The idea that children regarded climbing to be a rite of passage is further supported by exchanges among less-prolific climbers. See, for example, the following conversation.

I am standing on the ground below a tree. Kyle is on a branch, and Luke, a new child in our class, is below him, his hands holding on to a branch and his feet planted firmly on the ground.

"Luke can't climb the tree," Kyle says. Luke does not take kindly to this statement, despite its factuality.

"I am not little. I am not," comes Luke's frustrated reply. "I'm bigger than you," he adds. This is true. Luke, though younger than Kyle, is bigger. However, the fact remains that Kyle's full calendar year of climbing experience has given him a leg up—pun intended. As I write this, I remember that Kyle and I spent his first day at NOLA Nature School—by this time over a year ago—climbing the infamous Super Tree.

Kyle looks down at Luke from the branch.

"I got up," Kyle says with a small nod.

The statement is brief and effective. It seems that Luke understands what I perceive to be Kyle's implied, "I'm here, and you're not, so why don't we talk when you can get up here like me?"

The Multidimensionality of Photography

I have already mentioned how photographs give insight into the micro-moments that comprise otherwise unseen or overlooked experiences. Photographs are also artifacts that can be visited and revisited, with each subsequent visit inviting new or updated perspectives on and connections to the events they feature.

Here you'll find a series of images of climbing. As an ethnographer of this practice, it felt valuable to me to collect instances of this exploration that went beyond the written and transcribed.

As you look at the following images, I invite you to wonder:

What might these photographs reveal about climbing as a cultural practice and what children are taking away from it?

What do these images have to offer in addition to the words and stories listed above?

In this photo, Ian, William, and Laura are nestled in a large live oak. Climbing this tree was, I observed, an arduous task. When they made it to the top, I asked them if they wanted their journals, my adult goal to encourage the children in mark-making colliding with the children's desire to be in the tree. The children did want their journals, and they thoroughly enjoyed watching me try (and fail) to throw their journals up to them.

In these photographs, Daisy sits on a low branch of the Climbing Tree, her first attempt to climb it—to climb at all. As the youngest, newest, and physically smallest member of our class that year, Daisy often preferred to observe the world snuggled close to a trusted adult. Her interest in this rite felt significant.

Daisy secure and contented on the branch.

Minutes later, Daisy is still in the background on the branch while, in the foreground, Kyle writes in his journal.

Climbing, the photographs underscore, seems to be about more than just climbing itself. The rite of passage of climbing has its own set of social rewards that offset the inherent physical dangers of which the children are acutely aware. In the treetops, children have access to a protected interactive space that is inaccessible to adults. The photographs offer a visual representation of the story captured in the field notes, which read:

Part of climbing is also spending time in the tree. Resting, planning, observing, chatting, savoring.

And while it is possible to conjecture, it may be ultimately impossible to plumb the full depths of what a cultural practice may mean, even for members of the culture itself.

The children have been climbing. It's either the weather, the fact that winter has already divested the trees of their leaves, or the fact that a year plus at Nature School has lent treetops as much familiarity as the forest paths that we once frequented—whatever the case, the fact remains that it is a season for climbing.—Field Notes, February 2022

There are new experiences each day. Last week alone: Climbing Lauren's fort in the forest, Trey getting stuck, Faye's tumble from the low branch in the forest, Kyle's tears, Laura's bravado, and William's and Ian's boasts and fears existing side by side. Daisy's lift-off and firm declaration of loving to climb now because "I just do." Trey's declaration of his climbing abilities as a four-year-old. —Field Notes, March 2022

Lessons from Investigating Children's Right to Climb

✦ Images of Children and Childhood

In contrast to the other two contexts explored in this chapter, the dominant image of childhood at NOLA Nature School was in accord with my own deeply held beliefs. This meant that, unlike the other spaces, there was no tension between the institutional image of children and my own—a rare and wonderful situation. NOLA Nature School was and still remains a place that is open to a variety of ways of working with and being with children, such that I was able to enter fully into this work without reservation or worry about administrative censure or pressure.

✦ Inexhaustible Richness and Unique and Proximate Positioning

As with roughhousing, walking, show-and-tell, making messes, or sitting at a table with friends, climbing was a commonplace practice that I was able to consider more richly by looking through a new lens. By being close to climbing as it happened, I was able to listen in on conversations, trace threads between children's conversations and prior events across time and space, and document climbing with intention.

✦ Documentation as Ethnography and Advocacy

As the children in my classroom at NOLA Nature School were anywhere from one to three years older than those at the other preschool, and given the Nature School's lack of stringent institutional demands, my coteacher and I were able and encouraged to experiment with our methods of documentation. Of course there were occasions when we used language that families were familiar with to describe the children's days—the cooperation of climbing a tree together, for example. Yet most often this meant that we were able to be transparent in our communications with families and community members about our centering of what we read as the children's priorities for their lives each day. If on a particular day our curriculum, in its entirety, was climbing, we could celebrate this together, marveling at the richness that was.

CASE 4: LANGUAGES OF ENCOUNTER

In the Reggio approach, the term *language* describes a modality through which the child engages with and makes an imprint on the world. Materials, situations, and interactions all invite children to "speak" a "language." Through the use of these languages, children build up experiences that enrich their engagement with the world.

The framework that I call Languages of Encounter also emerged at a unique time in my teaching practice. That is, it sprung somewhere from the intersection of my own curiosities and from NOLA Nature School's institutional need. During my first year of teaching at the Nature School, I knew that I had a great deal to learn and harbored tons of curiosity about the processes of learning and creativity that I was observing. I felt, deep within my bones, that this sort of work was *right*. I had read books and research that seemed to confirm this. However, reading and a vague feeling only get one so far. Instead, I needed to feel it and know it for myself as an educator.

I also felt an obligation—the aforementioned accountability—to the families who were entrusting their children to my care. I wanted to be able to show them what was happening and to equip them, when they went beyond the boundaries of our own classroom, to share the rich reality of what was unfolding among the trails and trees with those in their lives and their children's future institutions. And so I strove to answer the questions: What are the mechanisms by which children are encountering the forest? What "languages" are the children using, and how do these look in our context?

Finding the Languages

I remember the day clearly. It was January 12, it was cold and wet from a recent rain, and that afternoon I had only two children. When it's cold and you're outside and it's raining on and off, the safest bet is to keep moving—and so we went on a Wander—a long hike where the wandering is the goal, a term borrowed from the *Coyote's Guide to Connecting with Nature* (Young, Haas, and McGown 2010). The children and I created a map; made our way past duck prints, a pond, and a sculpture; and then trekked over a bridge and through a field of early winter blooms. It was a magical day.

Louis points to the map as William adds a detail.

The in-progress map of the rainy day Wander.

William and Louis at the Memorial Fountain

Louis looks up the tracks using a field guide while William considers their placement on the map.

William adds some detail to a map.

As with many things, the impact is hard to realize in the moment. Over time I was surprised to notice how deeply and thoroughly the two children remembered this Wander. Of course I knew that children often have impressive memories, so the memory itself was less intriguing to me than my wondering at what this memory said about this child's sense of connection to the outdoors. On subsequent visits, Louis and William would show others around and make constant reference to the day we spent wandering about—it was foundational for the trajectory of the rest of our year and for my own understanding of the way that children were and could possibly move within natural spaces. In the following weeks, I identified at least six features—"languages" of the experience of our school that guided our time together, integrated from personal experience and *The Coyote's Guide* and inspired by Alison Clark's (2001, 2017) Mosaic approach and Sarah Pink's (2021) visual ethnography. These were Wander, mapmaking, journaling, memory, play, and photography.

After sitting with this list for some time, I began to wonder how I might learn more about the children's connection to the natural world through looking at each of these practices in depth. What could a one-by-one exploration of each one reveal about the ways that the children in our school were approaching their daily lives?

LANGUAGES OF ENCOUNTER	EXAMPLES
Wander	We amble down a forest path with nowhere in particular to go. We pause to look at a strange assortment of mushrooms at the base of a tree; we walk down a path and decide to look out for alligators. Finding none, we walk back to our classroom, spotting another group of children along the way.
Mapmaking	As we Wander, we decide to create a map. Children take turns drawing landmarks, writing letters or words or making other meaningful marks, and so forth. The map is stored in our book of maps.
Journaling	Children choose an event, idea, or object from their day to document in a journal.
Memory	Memory becomes evident when children refer to past events and make connections between those events and current events. For example, when a child references a friend's big fall from a tree that happened a year ago. Many memories—such as a Wander to an interesting place or a rare sighting—are collective landmarks.
Photography	Children take photographs of a place, space, group of children, or, really, anything they like. These photographs are printed and pasted in our classroom floorbook and become part of our ongoing conversations and discourse.
Play	When playing in the outdoors, children experience the multilayered joys of creating memories together, expressing themselves in play, and creating concrete memories of self-expression within the natural world.

Field Notes, November 2021 in the Forest (from my journal with the black cover)

Water Animal Classroom

Memory lives within spaces. Leo's hurt. Nick's bloody nose.

[When Trey said,] "The swing bonked me in the eye—a long time ago. Guys, it doesn't hurt anymore!" he reassures us.

A little farther down the page, my notes continue:

"Remember last year when I was four and I went that far and I fell?" [Louis says this as he runs into the swing, landing on his stomach and sending the seat shooting up in the air a few feet from the ground.]

I write: "#injury, but also increased competence. The change in ability."

The Benefit of An Ethnographic Approach + Mindset

In many ways, I consider Languages of Encounter to be the quintessential example of how an ethnographic approach to capturing the otherwise unseen moments of children's lives benefits the children, their families, and the institution and reinforces a strong image of the child. Formalizing and unpacking these languages helped give structure to and affirm our school's adherence to the emergent curricular framework we adopted. And, what's more, it proved to be a force for continuity of experience when, one day, things shifted.

Toward the end of the year I began Languages of Encounter, there was a shift in our relationship to the park. For a constellation of reasons, it became evident that our school would no longer be able to hold daily classes in the space, and while that realization was painful, it also left us with new questions, which Languages of Encounter as a framework was poised to investigate. How would the children's relationships to the natural world change and shift as a result of our new school status? Would the same Languages make sense in a different physical space that was less forested and more naturalized, where the outdoors is visibly human-made and human-managed? Ultimately, we faced an institutional identity crisis: How would we retain the special relationships, described and explored through these languages, in a new space?

Having this framework made making connections between our previous experiences and our new experiences easier. In the following table, I present some examples of what Languages might have looked like in the forest and in the city.

Facing page:

Away we go! Louis catches up to his friends who are a little ways down the street.

Wandering across a bridge in the forest.

A Wander down a city street.

LANGUAGE	IN THE FOREST	IN THE CITY
Wander	Wandering down a forest path.	Wandering down a city street and looking at cars, ongoing construction, posted flyers, and yards.
Mapmaking	Making a map of the forest paths as we wander.	Making a map of our neighborhood landmarks, such as the library, café, and bookstore.
Journaling	Journaling experiences/artifacts from the forest—leaves, trees, animals.	Journaling experiences/artifacts from the city—gardens, construction vehicles, physical places (e.g., storefronts).
Memory	Remembering when it rained so much there was a huge puddle of water around the base of the tree.	Remembering a wander through the neighborhood to the Spooky House.
Photography	Reflecting on the visual images of our time in various spaces and places.	
Play	Experiencing play for its own sake and as a place-based memory.	

Our Wanders, instead of following forest paths, now took us down city streets, though still bounded on either side by live oaks. Cracked sidewalks underfoot, construction crews sounding all around, sightings of neighbors taking in the day from a shaded porch, neighborhood cats to greet, new adventures . . . same language, different dialect.

We are walking down a street toward a coffee shop a block away. We begin the Wander with a single guideline—"We all stay what?" I ask.

"Together!" comes the reply, from most though not all of the children. It is, it seems, never all of the children who agree.

Along the way, we catch sight of trash cans and a cat that weaves its way through them to say hello to us. It gets close enough to touch.

A few steps down the road, we stop again.

The Wander was as slow as ever, intentional and child-led as ever, as connective as ever. To our acquaintance with plants and trees was added a familiarity with stoops and sidewalks, with houses and cats and shrubs, with ongoing construction—another artery of human life, no less place-based, no less relevant.

In the same way as it had in the forest, memory also anchored us to this new urban space. It became a thread that connected us to the concrete, the gardens, our slice of neighborhood. As our space changed, we documented its growth—the mulch we lined the lot with, the trees and shrubs that sprouted up in its place, the day a parent stayed with us to build an aqueduct. Each of these experiences created a new foundation upon which a new narrative of place-based relationship could be built.

Martin helped us to build an aqueduct.

Nearly a year later, Louis, too, made an aqueduct. He knelt in front of the rain barrel on a damp day and, as the water dribbled from the spout, arranged slivers of bamboo atop bricks and buckets, creating his own aqueduct.

"Just like my dad," he noted.

Indeed, just like his dad.

Louis takes a close look at the aqueduct.

Louis's dad, the year prior, working on the aqueduct with the children.

Lessons from the Languages of Encounter

By using this familiar frame of the languages of play, journaling, wander, memory, mapmaking, and photography to guide the way we spoke about and presented our curriculum to families, we were able to visualize the continuity between our program as it was and as it was becoming in ways that were grounded in our daily realities. Our program retained its essence. In many ways, the lessons in Languages of Encounter are amply evident above, in the children's connections to place, the formation of relationship, and the institutional sense of continuity that this lens provided our school. Yet for the sake of continuity and to connect them to the framework that has guided us throughout the book, I review them here.

✦ Images of Children and Childhood

Languages of Encounter is built on a foundation of children as multimodal, multi-talented individuals who can and do express themselves in and through a diverse array of possibilities.

✦ Inexhaustible Richness of the Day

The Languages of Encounter framework is grounded in the idea that the features of everyday life are inexhaustibly rich—that the same actions, over and over, time and again, help children travel with ever-greater intent, intensity, and depth down the paths of inquiry and discovery. The framework is intentionally sparse, the languages purposefully few, to underscore that in a few key spaces and activities there is what feels like boundless possibility for expression—children are speaking complexly in the small utterances, in the micro-moments, in what Jon Young, Ellen Haas, and Evan McGown (2010) call *core routines* and *keystone behaviors* through use of the basic materials and through the very act of engaging in life as it comes and through all of its evolutions.

✦ Proximity

Fluency in these languages was only possible through our repeated, up close, and personal interactions with children. This proximity allowed us to see the ways that these pieces of the day contained and developed stories with threads that extended throughout and beyond any single day.

✦ Documentation as Ethnography

In some ways, documenting the languages as ethnography was a natural outflow of my existing documentation practice. The languages are cultural rituals that hold meaning for the group of children. The languages reveal what is valuable within the cultural space of nature school, and by looking at children's engagement and living with the languages, we can see the ways they adopt, reinterpret, and shift cultural practice to suit their ends (or not).

✦ Advocacy

Advocating for children's lives is an essential piece of being an early childhood educator. To speak convincingly and compellingly about children's experiences, about what children know, need, desire and deserve, it is important that we learn new languages to describe their lives and use new lenses to look at the work they are already doing.

Through mastery of these languages, the children, in a sense, were also able to advocate for themselves. I argue that even though the children's behaviors might seem to have stopped short of fully actualized advocacy, their engagement in the forest and their reflections on their feelings, experiences, and play within it all constitute a convincing argument. These children were passionate about play and strove, using the Languages of Encounter, to show others the reasons behind their passion. As adults, we can take the children's actions as an argument in favor of their presence in public spaces *and* underscore the import of including children in decisions about such spaces.

Reflections

What does advocacy mean to you?

What are some needs, causes, and similar that you can see or imagine arising within your own context?

What ideas about children or practices with or related to them do you want to support, change, or challenge?

What are the concerns of those who have power and influence in your space? How do these concerns connect to the things you listed above?

How might the points made in the stories in this chapter have been less powerful without this close-up lens?

How, in the processes of advocacy, might you yourself be transformed along with the others you are trying to influence?

~ Chapter 6 ~

Learning from Ethnographies

☐ ☐ ☐ ☐

INTRODUCTION: WHAT CAN WE DO WITH ALL OF THIS?

Conceptualizing our work as ethnography helps us appreciate the complexity with which children are approaching life and the nuances of the richness that unfolds each day. It helps us advocate for children, speaking compellingly about their experiences with sensitivity and precision and in a manner that centers—or at least provides significant consideration of—children's priorities, perspectives, and motivations. While institutional demands may often be in ostensible conflict with this perspective, or certain features of it, it is in our own and the child's best interest to take this lens to their daily lives and experiences. In this chapter, I consider what we can learn from ethnographies and how we might incorporate ethnographic perspectives into our everyday places of work and care.

AN OPENNESS TO THE CHILD'S PERSPECTIVE

Turning ethnographic lenses on children's lives opens us up to the way a child experiences the world. Indeed, this is perhaps the primary benefit of using an ethnographic lens to document children's lives. While fully entering a child's world may be impossible, we can strive—as adamant teacher-researchers and field-workers—to assemble as clear a picture as we can of how the child is seeing life. We can ask questions such as these:

What does it mean to be a friend?

What does it really mean for this child to play with this set of blocks?

What does it mean to push a friend, to want to be tackled?

What does it look like to capture the world through one's own photographs?

These and the unlimited questions that surround us become possible for us to approach and even to begin to answer.

Another of the great beauties of an ethnographic perspective is that it enhances our understanding of our own positionality as educators and humans, and it is a constant reminder of our own situatedness with respect to the children. It requires remembering, consistently, that the way we see the world as adults is not necessarily the only way to see it and that we, even in our most well-intended moments, are coming to our interactions with a perspective that influences the way we see the world. This is not something to lament, but merely to remain aware of. We ask questions like these:

How are my questions affected by my interests?

How do my images of children and childhood form my framing for this investigation? This presentation of results?

INTERROGATING CULTURES: CHILDREN'S AND OUR OWN

Understanding our own positionality poises us to wonder whether children's developed and enacted cultures and practices are beneficial to them. Said otherwise, is what children are doing supporting a positive classroom climate overall? This is a point where we step back! So far, an important focus of our practice has been to inhabit the role of a participant observer who regards and respects children's actions and interactions, whatever they are, as informative, valuable, and important. While I wouldn't venture to say that this is no longer the case, this consideration of how a cultural practice may or may not be benefiting children is an invitation to inhabit our roles as nurturing adults in children's lives. We are not leaving behind our insistence on children's participation in meaning-making, but, instead, we are using the meanings we see children creating to inform the ways we support other facets of their lives as teachers co-constructing knowledge, as those supporting them in and through emotional conflicts and stress, as individuals who celebrate their joys, and more.

A critical feature of our role as educators is to move between inquiry and reflection. And, as we move between these, to wonder all the while *why* we are seeing what we are seeing. Said another way, we can take a look at the "capturings" we have collected over the extended course of our observations and interactions and wonder why we have seen what we have seen, and consider whether what we have seen is, ultimately, of benefit or not. We can ask the following:

How are the practices of the children's cultures affirming the children as a collective of individuals?

What are signs that a cultural practice is benefiting children?

What are signs that cultural practices, particularly within children's peer cultures, are not benefiting children—are maybe harming them or at least hindering their full expression?

For example, are the children depicted below reproducing a norm that builds community?

When the Rough Boys began playing their rough games, I began by observing. However, when the children started showing a lack of respect for one another's boundaries, it was evident that something needed to change. Hence the collective conversations documented in the previous chapter where I sat the children down and invited them, through multiple modalities, to consider their play more extensively. Ultimately, it seemed that the children's exploration of rough play provided them with opportunities to reflect on their and others' boundaries, and to express and process their ideas and emotions in a community of trusted friends. The fact remains that this may just as easily not have been the case. For example, had the children shown an inability to come together respectfully, we might have taken a different course of action. Meeting the children's need to connect in this way might have necessitated working with them to develop a new set of cultural norms that would be more conducive to their goals—a set of norms that might have included disallowing or severely restricting this sort of play. However, the children's desires to play, ability to reflect, and my own willingness to give them space all coincided to make it possible for the play to remain.

Indeed, this brings us to the next benefit of this ethnographic approach and lens to the life of the child: understanding children's priorities and goals for their relationships—wondering how, as the adults in their lives, we can support children in these goals.

CHILDREN'S GOALS

Every individual and culture has and holds a set of goals that are informed by and exert influence upon their culture and its attendant values. Viewed through a cultural lens, particularly in conversation with William Corsaro and others (Corsaro 1992, 2015; Corsaro and Eder 1990), we can consider ourselves to be ethnographers of children's peer cultures. As ethnographers of these peer cultures, we are deeply interested in these goals, and we consider it an important component of our work to uncover them.

These goals can exist in harmony with our adult goals, in tension with them, or even in direct opposition to them. Whatever the case, explicitly looking for and acknowledging the presence of children's particular cultural goals is valuable because of the habits of mind it invites us into. We remember, remember, and remember again that our way of seeing the world and our way of understanding the connection between the moments of the day and our broader visions is idiosyncratic and grounded in a particular experience. Of course, as educators, we maintain a degree of power over the children in our care. This power is not something that is ever possible to relinquish fully—however, I encourage us all to ask ourselves how we might share power with children. At any rate, in whatever context we find ourselves, we can make room for the children's goals at whatever scale feels most accessible. Ultimately, as with everything in early childhood, this boils down to relationship. Taking this close look at children's lives is a way of building relationships with them.

PROMOTING ETHNOGRAPHIC PERSPECTIVES IN SCHOOL

Ron, what do you do with all of those photos?

How do you have the time to do this sort of stuff?

Does it really make a difference?

I know that the perspectives offered over the course of this book are not the norm within most early childhood settings and spaces. Further, while I hope that the words and stories presented here have convinced you that this work is worthwhile, I also acknowledge that doing this sort of work comes along with its own set of challenges. I want to explore some of the challenges you might encounter in attempting to infuse the perspectives and practices outlined in this book into your day-to-day work with children and then offer some potential invitations to respond to these difficulties.

Challenge: Time Constraints

The reality is that as educators we face an abundance of constraints on our time, both in and out of classrooms. Further, these tight constraints are often exacerbated by conditions within the early childhood context. Difficulties with staffing and ratios, attending to unexpected emotional needs among the children, planning for daily and weekly activities, monitoring ongoing assessments and benchmarks, and coordinating school events and family communication are all ongoing considerations. Where can this sort of work fit in? Who has time for this?

✦✦ Invitation: Begin with a single practice.

In response, I recommend taking things slowly—starting with a single practice. What will work for you tomorrow? Next week? How can you take one little thing—or even half of something—and bring it into your lived experiences in your place of work?

For example, maybe you want to start off by taking a close look at children's activities in the art area. Think: How will you investigate this practice? Are there any curiosities you have already? How might what you already know influence what you look at or want to see? How might taking a close eye to a particular way of creating art or interacting with materials develop your appreciation for a practice that might be otherwise overlooked?

A group of two-year-olds is working with clay and liquid watercolors. A few minutes into the exploration it is amply evident that the liquid watercolors hold far more intrigue for the children than does the clay that is their substrate. Fingers dip into deep red, palms splash vibrant purple, and skin stains provide enduring testimony to the children's voracious exploration.

What does this practice, this dipping, reveal about the children's creative processes on this day? How might it connect with other trends we have been observing in the classroom? Is it—or does it carry precursors of—a new practice? Perhaps an interest in colors and mixing? An interest in exploring liquids?

✦ Invitation: Do your best not to hurry.

In addition to beginning with a single practice, I also encourage educators who are just beginning to explore the possibilities of this approach or building their own practices to give themselves time. Try out some of these ideas for a week or a month, and then take some time to reflect: What felt good? What resonated with you? What didn't? Why?

For all of us who work with young children, regardless of our context, there are times of the year—months or even seasons—that feel busy and, frankly, are busy. We have conferences, meetings, professional development, sick days, and on and on. Give yourself loads of time, and don't stress if you aren't able to do everything all at once. Do what works for you.

✦ Invitation: Build on what you are already doing.

One final recommendation I have to offer for time-constrained educators involves building on your current practices. Where can you weave in aspects of this approach into what you are already doing?

Can you add a sentence to your conference form? Frame a child's participation in a different way?

Is it possible to add another, different question or dimension to your observation forms?

Can you experiment with using different language to describe children's actions in a classroom newsletter?

As educators, we are already doing meaningful, worthwhile work! We should feel free to take creative and intellectual license to experiment with, finesse, and refine the ways we do it. And just remember, if you try something and it doesn't work, ask yourself why it didn't, and then resolve to try something new. Play, create, inquire, and imagine!

Challenge: Intersectional Roles

In early childhood contexts, we are often navigating a variety of roles. Not only are we teachers/caregivers/assessors with children, but in various places we are also providing before- or after-school care, facilitating enrichment activities for students, and maybe stepping in as an ancillary or even a primary administrator. Early educators are rightfully celebrated for our flexibility and willingness to serve and invest in our communities. This also, however, means that we are always being pulled in many directions. How can we focus amid everything we are doing?

Invitation: Respond to an issue or conflict.

Justifying this ethnographic, fine-grained approach is one of the foremost challenges of work of this sort. In the current climate of early childhood education and care, we are, rightfully so, increasingly aware of the urgent needs of children. There is, concurrently, an increasing consensus that we must address these needs and the inequities that produce them in our daily work. This is especially (and, again, *importantly*) the case in areas and spaces that can be considered "high need" on any level.

That said, this approach is a valuable way to begin exploring a response to a community issue or offering a richer or more detailed perspective on it. Begin with observation: What is the issue or tension? How is it impacting the community within your classroom?

After you have identified the issue at hand, you might look at the children's actions and interactions across time and space—where do their actions provide clues to ways that they might already have pieces of a solution or way forward? Document these moments and get specific about the places where you can identify actions or interactions that show indicators that the children have the tools to address this issue. This way you are able to underscore how, through your ethnographic perspective, you were able to discover and tap into a source of children's knowledge that otherwise you might not have seen.

This is especially valuable when you are responding to an issue or need that has direct impacts on children but where children's voices, perspectives, and experiences fail to be considered or collected—and it is a central component of Alison Clark's Mosaic approach (which invites children into occasions of collaborative meaning-making through multiple modes of creation) that, as acknowledged, is a significant inspiration for this book. Indeed, whether the issue is "hot button" or not, placing this work in explicit relationship with institutional-level conversations can help to give said issue some of the traction it might need to "stick."

 ## Invitation: Make it part of a professional development or team-building experience.

Another way to prioritize or fold this approach into your work in schools is to integrate it into an ongoing experience of professional development or vision setting. This way, not only do you invite educators and those working in your context to align on a set of practices and perspectives to foreground in their work, but you tackle, head-on and proactively, the (exciting) challenge of making these practices explicitly relevant to the work and life of your center. For example, during a professional development session focused on supporting children through transitions, educators can discuss and generate real-life case studies to explore how closely looking at children's experiences within classroom spaces has enabled them and others to respond to children in ways they would not otherwise have been able to.

Two further benefits of embedding this perspective within professional development experiences is that it becomes enshrined in the official discourse of your center and is reinforced as formative in nature. When we introduce an idea or concept during a professional development experience, it can become a topic of conversation and consideration across an entire school community. The ideas presented therein become part of the ether or atmosphere of a community, inviting everyone to engage with those ideas as feels most authentic to them. Furthermore, given that professional development workshops and trainings are typically intended to share principles, practices, and ideas that, enacted over time, lead to growth, placing these discussions within professional development contexts gives us an opportunity to frame them as trajectorial in nature—we send the implicit and explicit message that it is okay to try out these things.

Challenge: Institutional Norms

It is also valuable to consider how the perspectives of our institutions and the individuals within them will vary. After all, not every institution has a cohesive, coherent vision of children, childhood, or education. As educators know well, even between classrooms—and within classrooms—norms, practices, and ways of engaging and documenting work can vary. In fact, I would daresay that every educator has a way of doing things they are tightly wedded to—and while this is something that we must often be on our guard against lest we become too rigid, I want to invite us to think about our own preferences and tendencies as informative. After all, thinking about what matters to you gives you valuable insight into your own values. However, many educators and institutions are committed to norms or ways of being that do not respect or wish to consider the work of closely documenting children's lives from a child-centered perspective as valuable. For educators dedicated to work using the lenses we've looked at in this book, this poses another difficulty. Why, one might ask, would I work in this way if it isn't respected by those whom I work with or even within the place I work?

✦ Invitation: Build a community of practice and network of support.

The reality is that it is impossible to embark on this journey alone. In each of the vignettes, each of the stories here, I was working with or supported by not only a vibrant community of children but also a community of adults and educators who served as sounding boards, thought partners, and co-ideators in these endeavors.

- At my first school, my mentor teacher was incredibly supportive.

- In the pre-K, while the institution had less room to be receptive to my curiosities and ways of exploring children's lives, I was in the class with a lead teacher who was fully supportive of my curiosities.

- In the first preschool, I felt the support of my community of colleagues outside of the institution and drew upon the resources of my master's degree program cohort.

- At NOLA Nature School, I was constantly in conversation with dear teacher friends. I was fortunate enough to have a patient, excited coteacher from whom I learned a great deal about listening to, giving space for, and working with children, in addition to an extremely supportive administration.

The work we do is never singular nor isolated.

Finding and engaging with a community of practice—whether it is a formal group of educators who meet regularly or an informal cadre of friends that gather to chat and share ideas over lunch or while observing children playing on the playground—can be a wonderful way to build relationships with other educators and deepen your practice with new ideas as you share your insights with others. It also helps ensure that you do not get stuck in your own echo chamber, as there are many ways to see the same thing and many perspectives that can bring new and valuable hues to things that seem settled or static. Don't be afraid to engage them.

Challenge: Classroom-Specific Features

You must also consider classroom characteristics—and, possibly, contend with them—in striving to integrate a perspective that honors the small moments into your work. Every classroom is different. For example, some classrooms have children with interests or needs that require more extended periods of preparation or planning; other classrooms have blocks of the day that are reserved for a very particular sort of activity, which means that there are stringent boundaries on their time; and still others are parts of institutions where certain norms, practices, or experiences are nonnegotiable. In each of these spaces, taking a close look at children's lives—honoring the small, otherwise unseen and inexhaustibly rich moments—will look different.

In a place or space where the children don't have the sorts of opportunities as the children in this book—or even opportunities for much open-ended exploration or play at all—how can you begin to integrate this perspective and work in a way that (a) isn't too time consuming and (b) will deepen your practice and connect with your community in a meaningful way?

✦✦ Invitation: Experiment.

It is perfectly okay and completely reasonable to experiment. Given the dynamism of each classroom and early childhood context, being open to experimentation is critical. You will try. You will be overwhelmed. You will fall short. And you will also learn. You will succeed. You will learn more and see things in ways that you did not expect. The process is as daunting as it is enriching, and only through experimentation and creativity will you begin to find what works for you in capturing experiences and translating them for wider audiences.

REMEMBER: PROCESS

Remember that these invitations are not to be taken all at once! Take what works and leave what doesn't, holding space for the chance that this may change as you go forward. What works in one area may not work in another, what didn't seem like a possibility in one year can blossom into a beautiful practice the next, and a practice that you begin in one year may not become fully realized or fleshed out until many years down the line. This is wonderful—and normal!

I invite you to take some time, in this moment, to jot down some ideas of where you might start.

What challenges do you anticipate as you prepare to begin this work?

Where do you anticipate finding support?

While you may not be able to address every challenge right away, and while it is also unlikely that you will find unmitigated support, merely being aware of potential avenues of support and resistance will be useful as you attempt to incorporate these practices in the midst of busy days, each filled with its own joys, challenges, triumphs, and obligations.

Very often, in our well-meaning enthusiasm, we strive to implement a new practice, set of practices, or way of thinking, doing, and relating instantly. We want it all to happen at once. Now, we would think that being an early childhood educator would have endowed us with an appreciation for the process, right? Shouldn't we, as those who work with young children, be used to incremental progress toward a goal and understand that the goal is in the doing? Of course I am saying this in jest. Regardless of our orientation toward the idea of "process over product," the fact remains that we are often impatient or, at least, just wish we could be "there." In my conference forms some years ago, my coteacher Karin and I were feeling as if our assessments were causing parents an undue degree of worry over their children's abilities. We wanted to underscore that their children were in the process of developing and growing, and that we were fully aware of that. We decided to include a phrase that went something like "We want to acknowledge that the work of childhood looks many ways and unfolds over many years." It is a phrase I would like us all to bear in mind about the work of educating, and—more broadly—the work of being human!

Reflections

What is something that you think others in your space could stand to learn from ethnographies?

What do you envision will come easiest to you? What might be more of a challenge? Why?

What more do you want to learn, explore? What ideas might you want to revisit?

Where, tomorrow, might you begin your work?

References

Beatty, Barbara. 1995. *Preschool Education in America: The Culture of Young Children from the Colonial Era to the Present.* New Haven, CT: Yale University Press.

Clark, Alison. 2001. "How to Listen to Very Young Children: The Mosaic Approach." *Child Care in Practice* 7 (4): 333–41.

———. 2017. *Listening to Young Children: The Mosaic Approach.* 3rd ed. London: National Children's Bureau.

Corsaro, William A. 1992. "Interpretive Reproduction in Children's Peer Cultures." *Social Psychology Quarterly* 55 (2): 160–77. https://doi.org/10.2307/2786944.

———. 2015. *The Sociology of Childhood.* 4th ed. London: Sage Publications.

Corsaro, William A., and Donna Eder. 1990. "Children's Peer Cultures." *Annual Review of Sociology* 16:197–220.

Curtis, Deb. 2017. *Really Seeing Children: A Collection of Teaching and Learning Stories.* Lincoln, NE: Exchange Press.

Curtis, Deb, and Margie Carter. 2022. *The Art of Awareness: How Observation Can Transform Your Teaching.* 3rd ed. St. Paul, MN: Redleaf Press.

Edwards, Carolyn P., Lella Gandini, and George E. Forman, eds. 2012. *The Hundred Languages of Children: The Reggio Emilia Approach–Advanced Reflections Third Edition.* Norwood, NJ: Ablex.

Edwards, Carolyn P., and Carlina Rinaldi, eds. 2008. *The Diary of Laura: Perspectives on a Reggio Emilia Diary.* St. Paul, MN: Redleaf Press.

Einarsdottir, Johanna. 2005. "Playschool in Pictures: Children's Photographs as a Research Method." *Early Childhood Development and Care* 175 (6): 523–41. https://doi.org/10.1080/03004430500131320.

Emerson, Robert M., Rachel I. Fretz, and Linda L. Shaw. 2011. *Writing Ethnographic Fieldnotes.* 2nd ed. Chicago: University of Chicago Press.

Forman, George, Ellen Hall, and Kath Berglund. 2001, September. "The Power of Ordinary Moments." *Child Care Information Exchange*, 52–55. www.exchangepress.com/library/5014152.pdf.

Gray, Peter. 2013. *Free to Learn: Why Unleashing the Instinct to Play Will Make Our Children Happier, More Self-Reliant, and Better Students for Life.* New York: Basic Books.

Harvey, Peter F., and Annette Lareau. 2020. "Studying Children Using Ethnography: Heightened Challenges and Balancing Acts." *Bulletin of Sociological Methodology/Bulletin de Méthodologie Sociologique* 146 (1): 16–36.

James, Allison. 2001. "Ethnography in the Study of Children and Childhood." In *Handbook of Ethnography,* edited by Paul Atkinson, Amanda Coffey, Sara Delamont, John Lofland, and Lyn Lofland, 246–57. London: Sage Publications. https://doi.org/10.4135/9781848608337.n17.

———. 2007. "Giving Voice to Children's Voices: Practices and Problems, Pitfalls and Potentials." *American Anthropologist* 109 (2): 261–72.

Katch, Jane. 2001. *Under Deadman's Skin: Discovering the Meaning of Children's Violent Play.* Boston: Beacon Press.

———. 2003. *They Don't Like Me: Lessons on Bullying and Teaching from a Preschool Classroom.* Boston: Beacon Press.

Krechevsky, Mara, Ben Mardell, Melissa Rivard, and Daniel Wilson. 2013. *Visible Learners: Promoting Reggio-Inspired Approaches in All Schools.* San Francisco: Jossey-Bass.

Ladd, Gary W. 1990. "Having Friends, Keeping Friends, Making Friends, and Being Liked by Peers in the Classroom: Predictors of Children's Early School Adjustment?" *Child Development* 61 (4): 1081—1100. https://dx.doi.org/10.2307/1130877.

Lancy, David F. 2015. *The Anthropology of Childhood: Cherubs, Chattel, Changelings.* 2nd ed. Cambridge: Cambridge University Press.

Lawrence-Lightfoot, Sara, and Jessica Hoffmann Davis. 1997. *The Art and Science of Portraiture.* San Francisco: Jossey-Bass.

LeVine, Robert A. 2007. "Ethnographic Studies of Childhood: A Historical Overview." *American Anthropologist* 109 (2): 247–60. https://psycnet.apa.org/doi/10.1525/aa.2007.109.2.247.

Montessori, Maria. 1949. *The Absorbent Mind.* New York: Holt, Reinhart, and Winston.

Moran, Mary Jane. 1997. "Reconceptualizing Early Childhood Teacher Education: Preservice Teachers as Ethnographers." In *First Steps toward Teaching the Reggio Way*, edited by Joanne Hendrick, 210–21. Upper Saddle River, NJ: Prentice-Hall.

National Association for the Education of Young Children (NAEYC). 2022. *Developmentally Appropriate Practice in Early Childhood Programs: Serving Children from Birth through Age 8.* 4th ed. Washington, DC: NAEYC.

Paley, Vivian Gussin. 2004. *A Child's Work: The Importance of Fantasy Play.* Chicago: University of Chicago Press.

Pink, Sarah. 2021. *Doing Visual Ethnography.* 4th ed. Thousand Oaks, CA: Sage Publications.

Ritchie, Jenny. 2019. "Ethnography in Early Childhood Education." In *Oxford Research Encyclopedia of Education*, edited by Jenny Ritchie. Oxford: Oxford University Press. https://doi.org/10.1093/acrefore/9780190264093.013.532.

Rogoff, Barbara. 2003. *The Cultural Nature of Human Development.* New York: Oxford University Press.

Serriere, Stephanie C. 2010. "Carpet-Time Democracy: Digital Photography and Social Consciousness in the Early Childhood Classroom." *The Social Studies* 101 (2): 60–68.

Stacey, Susan. 2015. *Pedagogical Documentation in Early Childhood: Sharing Children's Learning and Teacher's Thinking.* St. Paul, MN: Redleaf Press.

Tuck, Eve. 2009. "Suspending Damage: A Letter to Communities." *Harvard Educational Review* 79 (3): 409–27.

United Nations. 2009. *Convention on the Rights of the Child* (July 1). www2.ohchr.org/english/bodies/crc/docs/advanceversions/crc-c-gc-12.pdf.

Yoon, Haeny S., and Tran Nguyen Templeton. 2019. "The Practice of Listening to Children: The Challenges of Hearing Children Out in an Adult-Regulated World." *Harvard Educational Review* 89 (1): 55–84.

Young, Jon, Ellen Haas, and Evan McGown. 2010. *Coyote's Guide to Connecting with Nature.* 2nd ed. Shelton, WA: Owlink Media.

Index